www.youtube.com/

@thequeenmaker

WWW.TIKTOK.COM/
@PRINCELLATHEQUEENMAKER

WWW.PRINCELLATHEQUEENMAKER.COM

The Game: 41 Shades of Men
©2023, Princella Clark
Self-Published
Princella@PrincellaTheQueenMaker.com

All rights reserved.
No part of this publication may be reproduced, stored in a retrieval system, stored in a database and / or published in any form or by any means, electronic, mechanical, photocopying, recording or otherwise, without the prior written permission of the publisher.

Princella Clark
P.O. Box 62795
Houston, Texas 77205
www.PrincellaTheQueenMaker.com

Introduction
10

The Software Program of The Human Being
20

The Hobo Sexual
47

The Lonely Man
61

The Destitute man
69

The Virility Validation Man
75

The Tax season man
81

The High Value Trick
84

The Family Man
88

The Emotionally Immature Man
95

The Sex Deprived Man
100

The Down Low Man
107

The Fellatio Man
116

The Jail Bird Man
120

The Step Mother Man
130

The Std Man
135

The Ego Boost Man
139

The Narcissist Man
143

The 'I Want Your' Child Man
149

The Green Card Man
156

The Let Me Make My Ex Jealous Man
159

The Pimp
163

The Business Man
168

The Political Man
173

The B.A.H. Man
176

The Murder Man
180

The Fetish Man
185

The Pro Black HoteP Man
189

The I'm Bored, Wife No Fun
196

The Insecure Sabotage Man
205

The Hospice Care Man
211

The Revenge man
216

The Rebound Man
229

The Poly Man
234

The White Girl Man
238

The Lesbian man
247

The Passport bro
251

The Midlife crisis man
256

The Save Face Man
262

The Only Fans Man
266

The Build-a-Bear Man
271

The "Pick Me" Girl Man
279

The Chess piece Man
285

Dark Psychology Personality types
288

Needs change, you're gone
316

"Life is a game to be played. You will either Play or get played. Those are your only two options."
-Princella Clark-

"It's not a thin line between love and hate, it's a thin line between caring and not giving a fuck."
-Princella Clark-

INTRODUCTION

In the wake of an ever changing reality in the area of male and female relationship dynamics, it has become evident there is a need for a reality check.

It doesn't take a genius to see the steep decline in marriage and the drastic uptick in divorces over the past few decades. Even Stevie Wonder can see the toxicity that prevails in modern times between men and women. The rise of the Manosphere has brought to the spotlight the angry, entitled and envious male. The so-called Feminist movement has brought to the stage capable women who seek to achieve and demand recognition for their humanity. These energetic places create an inverse relationship between the two sexes. The driving force behind the disruption is the rapid changes taking place in society. Although, humans are creatures of habit, they are also creatures of pleasure and avoiders of pain. The current shifts in social, economic and political infrastructures are creating unfamiliar painful feelings in one sex and unfamiliar pleasurable feelings in the other. Herein, lies the problem.

Society has long been under the artificial controls of patriarchal philosophy. A philosophy which deems the male to be of more importance and value than the woman. A philosophy which paints God in the image and likeness of a male, makes males superior to women and women's job to cater to his every need. Submission is her role and she is to allow man to do as he feels under the notion men are natural leaders. Last but not least, I t's a philosophy which tells women to help men under the guise of God creating her to be his help mate.

Because of this indoctrination, women have endured emotional, educational, spiritual, financial, physical and sexual destruction at the hands of males. They have also endured the same destruction at the hands of other women who have been weaponized against them. Despite this evident reality across the globe, women are still lost, confused and bewildered with how to have meaningful and mutually beneficial relationships with men. The obvious has yet to register with them; they shouldn't be trying to have these relationships. A mutually beneficial relationship is one that is founded upon effective communication, balanced giving and receiving, and is emotionally and spiritually fulfilling. This type of functional relationship would be in a state of homeostasis, the tendency toward a relatively stable <u>equilibrium</u> between <u>interdependent</u> elements, especially as maintained by physiological processes. However, women find themselves, lost, confused and bewildered in this department because they have often tried time and time again to do all that men have said they needed to do to achieve this state of homeostasis. Even in doing these things, they still feel themselves unfulfilled, drained and questioning their own sanity. Why?

What they fail to realize is they are not in <u>interdependent</u> relationships at all. They are in codependent relationships. What you will soon realize is relationships with males are rooted and founded upon codependency.

They are not created to work. Codependency destroys homeostasis.

    Through 25 years of consistent experience as a student of life and eight years of thorough introspection, connecting the dots from observation of the external world, I have come to understand, the world is out of natural order. I studied Cell and Molecular Biology at Louisiana State University in Shreveport. Amongst the core curriculum was Bio Statistics, Organic Chemistry I&II, Biochemistry, Cell Biology, Molecular Biology, Genetics, Algebra Based Physics, Calculus and Anatomy and Physiology. Through this training, I learned a great deal about learning, systemization, analysis, observation, theory, hypothesis formulation, proper research, the structure and language of the planet, universe and life. I was a high performing Psychology and Sociology student; naturally gifted in this area.

    I spent 8 years in the Army getting my commission as an officer. This training taught me the foundation of structure, systemization, following, leadership, mental deconstruction and reconstruction, organization, mobilization, planning and execution. I also spent 10+ years in Sales and customer service becoming top sales in each industry I worked. This training gave me direct experience and knowledge of human psychology and behavior.

As a former hip hop artist, I have spent time in the studio dealing with business and male psychology. Of course this is male dominated and you have direct experience with how they think feel and behave in these environments.

Each field I worked in was male dominated. I spent the majority of my life congregating with males. As a "tom boy" most of my friends throughout life were male. I have also been in romantic relationships with them. Because they felt comfortable with me, as a reflection of themselves, they revealed to me secrets about themselves they would never reveal to the everyday woman. These experiences and field knowledge has given me a level of expertise on this topic. I have combined all of this wisdom and knowledge to create a big picture for you to see clearly.

I conclude, women are disoriented with where they truly stand in relation to men. It is my belief that men are occupying a position on planet earth they were not naturally designed to occupy. Women have been lied to about the nature of men, their purpose in life, behavior, motives and psychology. The sad thing is women, by far and large, lack the desire to educate themselves on it. This desire to remain oblivious, foolish and dismissive of male existence fuels apathy and male resentment of women.

Women's belief systems about men have to be altered. Women are blamed for everything by the male because her current beliefs about males are destructive to the world, her children and most importantly herself.

Though her oblivion and romanticized thought patterns are not organically her fault, she is still seen as the problem due the nature of males seeing her as divine. Thus, the finger pointing. This oblivion also leaves her to point the finger back at him. It's an endless cycle of chaos and commotion. All of this is the doing of patriarchal philosophies.

Philosophies created by pillaging dominant white men. These men stripped women of their rights to autonomy in providing for themselves, sexual freedom, resource control, equity in the job market, equal pay and intellectual respect.

They put males in her place to run rampant with no controls except for those created by themselves. So, eventually, as time progressed, women found themselves fighting for equality. All due to the illusion and belief that she was coming from behind him to prove she is just as human as he. Unbeknownst to her, she has stepped down from her true position and allowed the male possession of what was divinely meant for her. In her state of oblivion and delusion, she is begging for him to take her power.

From the average male's perspective, who is not the creator of patriarchy, she is seen as taking a step backwards to lower herself to his level. He sees this because he knows his true position is of worshipping women and being behind them. He can not fathom why women would want to be like him or in his position. Subconsciously, the male knows the woman is his superior. However, the woman does not know he sees her this way. She is also unaware that his conscious effort to speak of his superiority is only to shift her perception of reality. He does this because her false perception of reality boosts his ego and his sense of importance.

You may ask, if he knows his true position is to be behind the woman, why won't he voluntarily kneel and submit to her? The answer is simple. Patriarchy did something most women have a difficult time doing; it stroked his ego and made him feel eternally important, valuable and needed. Open your eyes and see that patriarchy is a 180 degree flip of nature.

Due to this flipping of nature by the 1% who are in control, both the average male and female are confused about why the behavior of each other persists in the manner in which it persists. They are pointing the finger at each other, when the ruling class is responsible for altering reality to such a great extent. This confusion has caused great calamity in the world and mental destruction of both male and female.

I write this with the intention to reveal to women the true nature of man, his intentions and how his presence in her life affects her life as well as all life around her. I want to enlighten women on how to truly choose better.

To get the most out of this book, it is imperative you immerse yourself in the pre requisite, The 5 Components of Love. The 5 Components of Love teaches women what love truly is. The workshop, which accompanies it, shows and proves to women that men are incapable of love.

When you understand that men are incapable of love, you will no longer drain yourself to get something out of them that they are not capable of giving you. You will also understand men have a motive when they approach you and that motive is not to love you, but to use you.

It is my desire that women protect themselves from a lifetime of heartache and poor decision making.

In this book, I reveal 41 different types of men and what they pursue and use women for. In addition, I will outline the personality types and provide the power tactics of each one. Get ready to choose better.

P.S. NATURE, which centers the woman as the head, is humanity's religion. Patriarchy and Abrahamic Religions are man's religions which center him to ensure his survival as nature is not kind to him. To heal the world, we must return to MOTHER NATURE, MOTHER EARTH and the COSMIC MOTHER.

With love, sincerity and care,

Princella The Queen Maker.

CHAPTER 1
THE SOFTWARE PROGRAM OF THE HUMAN BEING

"IN THEORY, THERE IS NOTHING THE COMPUTER CAN DO THAT THE HUMAN MIND CAN NOT DO. THE COMPUTER MERELY TAKES A FINITE NUMBER OF OPERATIONS UPON THEM. THE HUMAN MIND CAN DUPLICATE THE PROCESS"

-ISAAC ASIMOV-

The greatest lie ever told to women is, men and women are equal, the same and/or men are capable of doing what women can do. Not only is this a lie, it is a deeply ingrained and strongly held belief of women. As a matter of fact, it is detrimental for women to hold the belief that men are superior to them. When you look out into the world and see the chaos you see, you may ask yourself, "why does the world look this way?" Would you be offended if I said, "Because women refuse to accept their rightful position on planet earth and are allowing males to destroy the world?" Men often scream, "you let him!" It may sound like the typical, "blame women for everything" that males scream, however, this has much rationale behind it.

First, we must understand the human make up. You have no functioning human without the most important organ…the brain. The brain is the central processing unit of the human. It is the computer and computers are programmable.

Secondly, each area of the brain is responsible for certain functions. These areas could be smaller or larger in volume which impacts functionality positively or negatively depending on the sex. It is important for women to understand that male brains function differently from female brains. Different does not mean good or bad, however, it does mean optimal capability or reduced capability.

Third, male brains are wired for competition and women's brains are wired to preserve social harmony. These functions are determined by the volume of the Orbital Frontal Cortex in tandem with the amygdala. This wiring gears men toward hierarchy, dominance and superiority— and women towards convergence, partnership and harmony. As a result of this propensity toward social harmony, women are more prone to promote the narrative of equality. Understand, this social harmony is inclusive of the male. Women will try to achieve this state of "equality" with the male via the use of methods such as the push, pull, beg and plead method. She pushes the male to achieve beyond his natural capabilities, she pulls him toward a more emotional connection, she begs him to do better and see her humanity, and she pleads for him to stop abusing her with his natural behavioral patterns which are toxic.

Women are constantly observing the unacceptable behaviors of the male. However, they lack understanding as to why he behaves in the manners in which he does. They see, through clear evidence, he is prone to produce children and abandon them. He is prone to violence and lack of emotional intelligence. Women push, pull, beg and plead for him to stop these behaviors. Even though they clearly see he has these deficits and the push, pull beg and plead method is failing, he is still seen as ranking above and superior to them. The sad thing about this is, it is women, themselves, defending these deficits and encouraging them to persist.

She is doing this blindly because women have been socially conditioned to see these deficits as traits of a high level being. She's also conditioned to believe women have been placed on this earth to sacrifice their lives to assist them with these eternal deficits. As a result, from a position of powerlessness, women began to use the push, pull, beg and plead method to convince the male to rise to a level of humanistic equality. The truth is, there is no such thing as equality and the male is not superior to women. Women, once upon a time, never pushed, pulled or begged males to do anything. They kept them in check and allowed nature to take its course. However, in more modern times, women have been manipulated into seeking equality.

The catalyst for women seeking equality was the creation of an artificial system which placed her economically, politically and socially behind the male. This gave her the illusion that she should be fighting to prove she was equal to who was actually behind her.

Women are moving in error, though, it is not entirely their fault.

Globally, women have largely been kept out of educational and critical thinking arenas. According to research, though girls have better literary ability and executive functioning, two-thirds of the 960 million illiterate people are women. As a result, women, specifically, are unaware of how the brain and mind functions.

The brain is a hardware computer that is programmable and uses software. The building blocks of this software flow in the following fashion: thoughts become words, words become sentences, sentences become paragraphs, paragraphs become philosophies, philosophies become actions, actions become habits, habits become character and character becomes destiny.

If you have acquiesced to new aged thinking, you are probably familiar with the book, *The Secret,* and the concept of, *The Law of Attraction*. These concepts purport the way you think affects your reality; the way you believe affects your reality. All you have to do is change the way you think because that is why you experience what you do in life. Have you tried this? Did your life change for the better? Most likely the results were negligible.

People have tried to implement this concept into their lives with very minimal results because it leaves out a critical element. The reprogramming process is not simply just changing your thoughts, it is about changing the core program. The brain is a computer and a computer runs on software. This software is a program of the brain and is not just a simple thought. The software of the brain is philosophy which is coded by language; in this case, English. In these modern times of lackadaisical efforts, we have created a modern day Tower of Babble. We are now too lazy to define the words we utilize everyday and instead make up our meanings to words that predate our existence. Therefore, to ensure this book conveys the message it is intended to convey, we will define, within theses paragraphs, the meanings of critical words being used. It is important to know the denotative definition of the words we use because these words are the building blocks of the software program that is creating your undesirable reality.

Google defines philosophy as a theory or attitude held by a person or organization that acts as the guiding principle for behavior. Guide is "to direct or have an influence on the course of action on someone or something." Theory is "a supposition or a system of ideas intended to explain something." Idea is a thought or suggestion as to a possible course of action.

So, in other words, you hold ideas or suggested thoughts about things that direct or have an influence over your actions and behaviors. <u>Influence</u> is the capacity to have an effect on the character, development, or behavior of someone or something, or the effect itself. The second context of the definition is 'a person or thing with the capacity or power to have an effect on someone or something.'

In other words, the ideas and theories you hold about things, have a direct power over your behavior, actions and decision making. These ideas are the program/software of your mind which is philosophy.

Several philosophies of the world have brainwashed and socially conditioned women to sacrifice themselves, ultimately, for the male's survival. These anti-natural philosophies were created and pushed by men.

The ideas within these philosophies are not your ideas; they did not originate with you. They are unnatural, manufactured and completely fabricated.

If you were raised as a Christian, this line should sound familiar to you, "Train a child in the way he should go and when he grows old he will never depart." This is Proverbs 22:6 highlighting indoctrination. To indoctrinate is to teach (a person or group) to accept a set of beliefs uncritically. To accept a belief UNCRITICALLY means you are to accept a belief without asking questions. Belief is defined as "an acceptance that a statement is true or that something exists." To believe means you have accepted concepts, ideas and information as true without investigation. The root word of indoctrinate is doctrine. A doctrine is a belief or set of beliefs held and taught by a Church, political party, or other group. You were given these ideas by your parents first and then reconditioned by an artificial society. You did not question your parents, you did not question your church, you did not question any of these philosophical ideals that you strongly believe in. Yet, you hold strong to them and fight tooth and nail to keep them. You've attached your ego/personal identity to them and became one with what has strong potential and evidence of being flat out lies.

To teach, coach and train is the process of programming the human CPU. Studies show, when babies are born, they've already acquired knowledge about language, food preferences, and emotions. A baby's hearing develops around 24 weeks in the womb, which allows them to learn the sound of their mother's voice and be able to recognize her native language. Indoctrination is not nature, however, it is nurture. To nurture is to condition one to adapt to social expectations. This nurturing is intended to manipulate behavior and control human nature.

We say, "human nature" however, it's simply nature as animals and insects behave in very similar patterns in a natural environment. Humans are simply another species of animal. What makes humans different from other species is the prefrontal cortex. This region of the brain simply makes humans aware of their existence. So, what is the critical urgency and need to control nature? The urgent need is felt by man because nature does not support the existence of males. In nature, males are expendable. Females rule and males risk failing at survival of the fittest. Males have to be the fittest to survive and nature needs very few of them. Men do not like nature and feel it is their ultimate duty to control nature's forces. Nature is known as MOTHER NATURE, MOTHER EARTH. This urgent fear of not surviving is why men dominate the realms of philosophy. It is the key to controlling nature and the world. It is the key to ensure his survival. It is the reason why you were conditioned to worship man.

Have you noticed philosophy, sociology and psychology are the fields that don't pay much in this world? Why? Because they do not want to incentivize and encourage you to discover the areas that have allowed them to govern and control the world. These areas encourage you to put two and two together. When you research history, you will find that women have been largely excluded from it and overshadowed by males. Men have used philosophy to control women's resistance to male insemination. Men have used philosophy to make women worship and pursue them. Men have used philosophy to confuse women and get them to voluntarily lower their defenses and allow them to run recklessly around the globe. They have used philosophy to make it acceptable to murder women and engage in sexual abuse of them and her children.

How? Under the guise of sacrifice to God and marriage. King James is the author of a book titled, _Demonology._ You've heard of him. He is also the author of the King James Version of the Bible. In Demonology, all you had to do was accuse a woman of being a witch and it detailed instructions on how to confirm if she was or not. The test consisted of tying together her hands and feet and throwing her in a lake. If she rose to the top, she was a witch and would be stoned to death. If she sank and drowned, oh well, guess she wasn't a witch. This was one of the philosophical ways women were murdered by males.

Have you ever questioned why it was ok for prophet Mohammad to marry 9 year old Aisha or why it's ok for families to sell their daughters to men under the idea of "marriage?" Have you ever questioned why society makes a big deal out of women desiring marriage? If you're heavy in these ideals, you most likely have not. Possibly, for fear of being ostracized or fear of burning in hell. This is because males have created an artificial environment ruled by philosophies they created to support their existence, fulfill their lower natured desires and ensure their survival. They need women to believe in philosophies that make it easier for males to attach themselves to them; especially, for what his biology wants him to get, youth. Currently, in Afghanistan, the poor and resource depleted environment has families selling their pre-pubescent daughters to men in their 50's and 70s! Imagine a 50 and 70 year old man buying kids to have sex with! This should infuriate you. Afghanistan is under Islamic doctrine.

It is necessary for you to understand, the behaviors of people can be attributed primarily to their philosophical program or lack thereof.

To more clearly understand what is and is not a philosophy, let's delve further into the meaning of theory since it is the foundation of what makes up a philosophy.

To help you understand, it is worth repeating the definition of theory again accompanied with another definition to consider, science. Theory is a system of IDEAS intended to explain something. Science is defined as, the intellectual and practical activity encompassing the systematic study of the structure and behavior of the physical and natural world through OBSERVATION and experiment.

Now, let's consider the following example of both science and theory. With science- you OBSERVE and SEE with your own eyes that women give birth and experience pain in the process, right? You also see that she has a menstrual cycle, right? If you don't see that, I am going to assume you are blind. If you do see that, congratulations, you have 20/20 vision. You qualify to fly an aircraft! This is the observable behavior of the natural and physical world which you are part of. This is science. This is fact.

So, if that is science, what is theory? Theory is a system of IDEAS USED TO EXPLAIN SOMETHING. So, what system of ideas is used to explain the science of women experiencing pain during child birth and menstrual cycles?

The idea that Eve sinned against God and was cursed as a result. The very first question you should be asking here is, "whose idea was it to explain this science in this way?" The second question you need to be asking is, "What sin?"

Are you afraid to ask questions? If you are, could it be that you were bullied by your parents or religious institution to not question "God?" Remember, indoctrination is teach (a person or group) to accept a set of beliefs uncritically. Critical thought is the process of involving the objective analysis and evaluation of an issue in order to form a judgement. What does it mean to judge? To form a conclusion about something. "Judge not lest ye be judged?" Does that sound familiar? Matthew 7:1 Another bible verse telling you not to think and form rational conclusions. They were successfully able to indoctrinate you with the use of fear. Fear is the number one control mechanism. Do you understand that asking questions is the process of critical thinking? To think critically you must ask, "who, what, when, where, why and how" questions. When you asked these questions as you naturally would as a child, you were conditioned not to. We will not continue this fear pattern in this Aquarian age of enlightenment, knowledge and technology, okurrr? (in my Cardi B voice.)

So, I will ask again, "whose idea was it to explain this science in this way?" Would women condemn and castrate themselves? Is the Bible or Koran written by women? Are any of the books headed by women? NO, NO AND NO. These were the ideas of men. What is sin? HUMAN NATURE! Why is human nature a sin? Because it does not favor the male and limits HIS nature of what he desires to do for his pleasure, ego and survival. Because nature favors women, the male must control nature and the woman.

How did he do this? Through the use of violence, fear and philosophical indoctrination.

Theories are the foundation of philosophy. So, what type of theory is Eve sinning and what philosophy is it the foundation of? Religious philosophy! Religious philosophy is NOT based in fact nor is it based in nature. It is an artificial program intended to govern and control human nature for male benefit.

So, who are the creators of this program? To answer this question in more depth, we must understand Maslow's Hierarchy of Human needs. At the very base of the pyramid, exists the physiological needs of all humans and animals. This is our primal/animalistic nature. The animal nature is the CORE and foundation of the human make up. It is our raw and natural self, not contaminated, by an artificial program. Humans are animals first, foremost and primarily. In the root word of PRIMAL AND PRIMARY is PRIME.

Primal is defined as relating to an early stage in evolutionary development. Original, initial, early. 2. Essential; Fundamental

Primary is defined as of chief importance, principal, main, key, prime.

Prime is defined as first importance, main. The main part of our make-up is physiological and that comes first before anything. This is nature—MOTHER NATURE. Our physiological needs consist of food, water, sleep, sex, excretion and breathing. These things are essential to our existence. When these needs are not met, people will get them met by any means necessary. By any means necessary means to forgo the concept of morality, ie, what is right or what is wrong to do. Morality does not exist at the base of the pyramid.

The next step on the hierarchy is Security. At this stage, personal security, health, resources and property are a focus. Also, security of morality exists here.

You may be wondering, how can security of morality exist here, if I previously stated that morality is not created on the bottom of the hierarchy of human needs. This is simple. Before, you incarnated on the planet, your parents and society began programming you with philosophies and morality which begins to become part of your ego, individual identity. Under the first law of nature, the law of self preservation, exists for the protection of one's ego, self identity.

The Next step is "love" and belonging. If you have attended The Love, Men and Manipulation Decoded Workshop previously The 5 Components of Love Workshop, you know this stage is NOT "love' and belonging, but emotional bonding and belonging. At this stage, your ego/self identity needs validation. You need to feel as if you belong somewhere. These are lower nature, lower self, self preserving, deficiency needs.

At the top of Maslow's Hierarchy of Human Needs is self actualization. This is where the least amount of people exist on the pyramid and where the least amount of conscious and unconscious functioning happen within a single person. This stage is where problem solving, morality and philosophy becomes the priority of a human's existence. Philosophy is created at the self actualization stage and morality is a by-product of that creation. Those people push the philosophies they create down to the people at the bottom of the hierarchy of human needs and programs the neuro networks in their brain.

It is said that humans only use 10% of their brains; the brain is more capable than humans are consciously aware of. This is in part to do with the reality people are on auto pilot. The brain of the average person is not used to think. To think is to employ one's mind rationally and objectively in evaluating or dealing with a given situation. Most people do not think. Most people do not ask, "who, what, when, where, why or how questions." They do not investigate. They do not process information through objective lenses. They simply believe what they hear or what makes them feel good. Therefore, what you believe is the act of thinking, is nothing more than preprogrammed pathways and neuro networks established by the software known as philosophy.

The English language is important to understand for those who have it as their primary language or native tongue. This is important as language is the building blocks of the philosophical software just as amino acids are the building blocks to proteins and life. When you understand science and break down DNA, you will understand like your English language, there is a language and sequence used to build the foundations of human life.

All languages have a system and a structure to it just as C++, an object-oriented programming language, used by software developers or the amino acid sequence for an essential protein used by your biological system.

Since this book is written in English, you need to understand the basics and the fundamentals of this programming language for the development of the software/philosophy on which your human computer runs. This is why I have focused on providing the denotative definitions for the most important words in this book.

The English language is a language constructed with the use of morphemes. Morphemes have a prefix, base and or suffix. Each one of these individual components of a word has a meaning.

Ism is a suffix. This suffix is defined as a distinctive practice, system, or PHILOSOPHY, typically a political ideology or an artistic movement.

It is important to note, that IDEOLOGY is a key word in the definition of ISM. Ideology is defined as a system of ideas and ideals, especially one which forms the basis of economic or political THEORY and policy.

Another important word is ideal. Ideal is defined as satisfying one's <u>conception</u> of what is perfect; most suitable. Existing only in the imagination; desirable or perfect but not likely to become a reality.

Any word ending in ISM is a philosophy or a system built around a philosophy which is a system built around ideas of a perfect or more suitable world. The ISMs and philosophies that you are programmed with, are ISMS and philosophies created by males. So, I have a question. Who do these ISMs and philosophies make a perfect and more suitable world for? Males

RacISM is a philosophy or a system built around the ideas of race practices. Capital-

ISM is a philosophy or a system built around the ideas of capital.

Social-ISM is a philosophy or a system built around the IDEAS of social practices.

Other ISMs, communism, feminism, spiritualism, Egoism, Classism, and Fascism.

The suffix -IST is defined as "a Follower of a distinctive practice, system, or philosophy, typically a political ideology or an artistic movement." Do you consider yourself a capitalist, socialist, feminist, or any -ist? Then you are a follower of someone else's ideas that govern your behavior. You are running on someone else's program.

Patri- is a prefix that means FATHER. -Otic is a suffix that denotes a relationship to an action, process, state or condition. So, if you are PATRI-OTIC, you are in a state of FATHER processes and conditions. Father, represents the male.

Another significant suffix is -archy, which is defined as abstract nouns for types of "rule", "government, or social influence.

This means a monARCHY, oligARCHY, and PatriARCHY are forms of rule, government and or social influence that has POWER over human behavior.

Patriarchy is defined by google as a system of society or government in which men hold the power and women are largely excluded from it. Patriarchy defined by the definition of both the prefix and suffix is a father rule, government or social influence. According to U.S.News, despite white men comprising only 31% of the population, 97% of all republican elected officials are white and 76% are male. Of all Democratic elected officials, 79% are white and 65% are male.

Based on the numbers of this government structure, the United States is a Patriarchal society because the "father/male" has rule, governmental control and male social influence. Which also means, the philosophies which govern the behaviors of the citizens are patriarchal in nature. As a woman reading this book, please recognize that you are NOT A MALE. Therefore, your behavior being completely influenced by males has taken you away from what it means to be a woman.

The religious philosophy mentioned earlier is patriarchally rooted. Christianity is part of the Three Abrahamic Religions, Christianity, Judaism, and Islam. Abraham means the first patriarch.

If you understand all the philosophical programs are male created, male and masculine dominant, you will understand the core of the program when you begin to understand the nature of male and his psychology.

The male sex does not love, he does not think, move or operate on an abstract concept of love. The male's nature is self preservation. He can not operate outside of this realm, the realm of the lower self. If you find a male who can, please understand he is of the EXTREME minority.

The male is only concerned with his personal survival at all costs, therefore, rendering it extremely difficult for him to transcend this realm. To ensure his survival, the male's brain is quickly triggered to competition. This competitive mentality is the driving force behind his desire to place women and all things into submission. This fact of male nature is the foundation of all patriarchal philosophies and programs. The male has incorporated his being and psychology into ALL philosophies created by and governed by males.

This is poisonous and detrimental to life, nature and women. When women are infected with this viral software, she becomes a powerful weapon used to destroy herself, her offspring, nature, society and other women solely for the purpose of ensuring male survival—male survival of his physical, mental, emotional, and financial position on planet earth.

It is this programming software that has caused China and India to overpopulate their region with 70 million more males than females. This caused and is causing major cataclysmic problems of a gender imbalance that has rippled an effect throughout the entire planet.

Now, you understand the programming software of the human mind, it is time for you to see that every single male who approaches you as a woman is approaching for a hidden agenda rooted in serving his survival needs.

In this book, I give 41 different types males and what they pursue and women for, their tactics, and some common phrases and lines you will hear. For some, I will also provide links to video admissions and evidence.

Now, you can be truly empowered to choose better.

No philosophy that goes against the natural flow of nature is a sufficient ism or system. They will all produce effects that will be riddled with problems for humanity, animal and plant life.

"Nature is the TRUE RELIGION of woman"
                    -Princella The Queen Maker-

CHAPTER 2

THE HOBO SEXUAL

"Housing is absolutely essential to human flourishing. Without stable shelter, it all falls apart."

-Matthew Desmond-

In 2017, a woman by the name of Nakita Nicci wrote an article that has sense given birth to this type of pursuant, The Hobo-sexual. In her article, she defines a hobosexual as a "person who dates you with the sole interest of having a place to stay, not a genuine or romantic interest."

If you have already read, The 5 Components of Love and attended the workshop associated with it, you already know men are not capable of love and a romantic interest is a delusion. Romantic by Google definition is defined as 1. conducive to or characterized by the expression of love. 2. Of, characterized by, or suggestive of an idealized view of reality. To connect the dots and give you the big picture, seeking an expression of love from a male who is incapable of love is a delusion in both senses of the word. To idealize (create a perfect world in one's imagination) reality is delusion in and of itself. Delusion is defined as an idiosyncratic belief or impression that is firmly maintained despite being contradicted by what is generally accepted as reality or rational argument, typically a symptom of mental disorder.

Many women have a habit of explaining or rationalizing away pure and blatant evidence in reality that men do not love and are not capable of it everyday to maintain the poisonous patriarchal program installed into their minds. Everyday she resists reality, she does not process the blatant truths men tell her everyday such as, "men are territorial!" "We don't love like a woman does" These are blatant truths directly from the horses mouth that men are incapable of love.

1. Love is completely absent of territory and ownership. Love is FREE, not in the context of giving away or accessibility but free in the context of inhibition. 2. There is no such thing as a woman's love. There is only one love and men are not capable of it. They tell you everyday they use you for your youth and beauty by verbally telling you that you are only desirable to them between certain ages. This is not love, yet women will try to persuade themselves to see it as some form of love anyway even though the behavioral evidence shows destruction of human life, self esteem, confidence and autonomy. Women are forcing themselves to behave against their biological program to uphold a psychological program that renders her with a clear mental DIS-ORDER.

I use dis-order in that manner because the biology always comes first as it is primary and the foundation of human make up. Psychology comes second. Those who place the psychological program before the biological program are out of order, thus creating a mental dis-order.

The correct order is to analyze everything based on the biology first and foremost, then, secondly, the psychology. This way you can clearly see where the error of this world lies.

Men are the sex who is trapped in a survival nature on Maslow's Hierarchy, deficiency need zone. That is his biology and is what ultimately drives his behavior. The philosophies he has created were created in this zone to support this zone.

Therefore, when a man approaches you, you should know, unequivocally, he is approaching you for a reason that is rooted in male reality, deficiency and need fulfillment. He can not approach you on higher level growth needs because those are based in higher philosophical reasons that are not the primary function of a male.

Males are codependent by nature and have a difficult time existing independently of women. This does not have an inverse effect in relation to women. If you meet a man who operates independently of women, he is an exception to the rule and part of a very small percentage of men. Women on the other hand can function and do function purely within themselves and achieve life goals independently of a male partner.

Women typically live alone in their apartments or homes. She has a stable environment where she can lay her head, cook her meals and raise her children if she has any. Men are, by large, displaced if they are not living with a woman. This could be a female relative or a stranger whom he targets for the sole purpose of living in her space.

A 2007 Study shows that living alone is a risk factor for mortality in men but not women. Another study shows that men who suffer two or more breakups or live alone suffer from higher levels of inflammation. This evidence indicates that it is an ever pressing need for a man to cohabitate with a woman. In addition to that, men are generally lazy by nature and have to be forced to provide for themselves. So, many of them take the route of using their penises as a tool and weapon to conquer the mind of a woman to sift out his primary need.

In this case, it is a place to stay.

I was recently sent a post from a social media platform by an anonymous woman which describes how she was bamboozled by the HOBO SEXUAL. The post reads as follows, "I was looking for love; he was looking for free housing. We met on Tinder, his name was King. My first-date idea was to meet up for coffee. King offered to cook for me in my home. He was fine and I was lonely so I agreed. King showed up, chocolate, bald, fine as hell and empty-handed; he cooked the food I had in my fridge. We ate French toast and eggs.
"You didn't bring food to cook?" I asked. King shot back, "am I supposed to buy groceries on a first date?!"
We had a great conversation and amazing sex. King deactivated his Tinder account in front of me and he spent the night. The following morning, King tried to stay in my home while I went to work but I refused.

The next night, King came back to my home (uninvited) and we watched Netflix. King brought liquor and we had amazing, drunk sex. He spent the night. And the next night. And the next...

For two months King remained in my house. His sex was top-tier and his conversations were amazing. King wanted marriage-with me. He wanted a large family-with me. And he wanted to support my dreams. But the sum of King's parts didn't equal the whole. Conversations and great sex don't pay my bills. In fact, my bills have doubled. Also, King splurged on himself but bought nothing for me. For example, he had a $350 pair of shoes arrive at my house, but he didn't offer to help me with the bills.

I mentioned to King that I couldn't afford cable and groceries for two, so I may have to let cable go.

Him: "Wow. How did you afford it before?"

Me: "I'm buying double the groceries and toiletries now."

Him: "Cable won't cut you off until you're a few months behind...let it ride."

Me: "Or, you could pay it this month"

Him: "Am I your daddy? Am I supposed to pay your bills?! Or am I supposed to do something else?"

King's "something else" was his amazing sex. King lived in a hotel before we dated, so I guess I'm his new hotel. In a moment of clarity, I told him I couldn't afford for him to stay overnight every day.

King said casually, "You know once I receive mail here, I'm legally your roommate?" He smiled. My heart sank to the floor.

I had a mooching stranger in my bed and I was defenseless. It's my fault; I told too much, too soon. King knew I didn't have any strong men in my life to throw him out. I'm an only child. No big, bad, uncles or brothers to protect me. No dad to come to my rescue.

And as a Black Woman, I understood that if I called the police, the situation could become deadly for both of us. The only way I could get this man out of my house was to drive him out. I decided to fake my own eviction; it took 3 painful days.

I paid my rent. I bought a burner phone, then I created a fake eviction notice with the burner phone's number on it, just in case he called. I slapped the notice on my door. (King didn't call the number, but a neighbor did; she said: "Leave that sound lady alone. You should be evicting the people next to me, they got the whole floor smelling like weed.")

I returned from work and showed King the eviction notice. I asked if he had money to help me out because I was about to be homeless.

Him: "I thought you were independent. Why you changing on me? You lied. You don't have your shit together."

Instead of cuddling with me, king was back on Tinder. We never had sex again.

On the third day, I put my cable service on pause (and told King that it was shut off.). I paid the janitor $20 to shut off the electricity to my apartment after I left work. King texted me: "yo! Power's off!" I responded.: "Oh no! Can you pay the bill!?" He left my message on read.

On my way home from work, I braced myself for the grand finale of packing my things and moving out. But, when I got home, King was already gone. I texted him. "Where are you?! I need help packing. Where are we gonna stay tonight, King?"

-message left on read-

If I'm honest, it did sting to realize that King wasn't really into me. And, yes, I'm jealous knowing that he's curling someone else's toes right now. But damn it feels good to have my bed and my castle all to myself once again. Farewell my dear king."

In December of 2020, I ran across a video of a hobosexual explaining the techniques he used to move into a woman's place. Here is the Link below.

https://fb.watch/hotsiGHEa5/

In this video, he speaks about using his penis as a weapon or tool to conquer the mind of the woman. Once he has given her "mind blowing" sex, he then falls asleep on a day she has to go to work. He states, "if she wakes up and leaves without telling you to leave, then just don't ever leave."

Men have a motive when they approach you. That motive is always to have you fulfill a critical need. Men operate on the bottom echelon of Maslow's hierarchy. This is the echelon of SELF preservation. This echelon consists of, food, sleep, water, sex, excretion, security, housing, self esteem, emotional bonding and belonging. These needs are in a constant deficit with males.

When they approach you, they are seeking to meet one of these needs. These needs are in constant rotation.

In this case, the male needs security and housing. Once this need is met, he will begin to seek a relationship with another woman to fulfill another need which he was not looking to be met or filled by the housing woman.

Look for the following signs that you are dealing with a Hobo-sexual

1. How much time does he have on his hands? Is he always available? If he has plenty of time to dedicate to you this is a red flag.

2. Is he on dating apps? If so, how many and how long? A person who is constantly on dating sites and multiple ones at that are looking for something specific.

3. Who does he currently reside with? If he says, anywhere but alone, this is red flag number one.

4. Does he pay his own bills at a place that is leased to him?

5. Is he employed? Hobosexuals can be employed. As a matter of fact, many are employed. Being employed with no place of his own is the red flag because typically this person will move into your place and then quit his job and pretend he can't find another.

Understand that males are lazy by nature. Sexual expression in the physical drains their energy and desire. On top of that, most of them have no higher purpose. So it is easy for them to lay around, waste time and seek a woman's care to preserve themselves.

How to test the waters:

1. Ask to spend the time at his place. Pay attention to any objections and delays. This will tell you he most likely either lives with someone or does not have a place of his own. If he does this, simply say to him that I'd prefer to be invited in your world and if not I don't think I can move forward. He will do one of two things, a. Gaslight you and accuse you of being petty or something along those lines, b. Play the longterm waiting game to have you questioning whether or not you're being too harsh or unreasonable. Watch for both signals. None of that matters. Does he take you to his place? If not, do not buy all of the nonsense that follows to justify why you can't go to his place.

2. This man will often insist to come to your place. He will typically ask you within the first conversation where you live. This is a question to determine

proximity. Many can ask this question and not be hobosexuals but a hobosexual will not leave this question out so it must be considered as a check mark in addition to other flags.

3. See how frustrated he becomes when you continue to refuse to allow him to come to your place.

You must play the extended waiting game.

You do not want a leech living off of your hard earned work and money.

My advice: Don't let him eat up your baby's Fruit Loops and don't let him stay the night.

CHAPTER 3

THE LONELY MAN

"And the Lord GOD SAID, IT IS NOT GOOD THAT A MAN SHOULD BE ALONE..."

-GENSIS 2:18 KING JAMES VERSION BIBLE-

❖

If you have been monitoring the climate of social media these days, you should be quite familiar with a popular scare tactic men use for women, "You're going to be single and die alone with cats." It is interesting how men often claim, 'men and women are not the same', yet believe the fears they have as men are the same fears women have. Projection is a common behavioral pattern for males who so desperately need to protect their egos.

According to research performed at Copenhagen Aging and Midlife Biobank, men who experience two or more breakups or live alone are at greater risk for inflammation. This is not the case for women. There are many confessions of men stating their reasons for settling with women and many of them are centered around their fear of being alone.

Here are a few quotes from men who confessed on 'Whisper.'

"I settled in a relationship I'm not fond of because I fear my early baldness will keep me from ever having a wife, much less the girl of my dreams."

"When I look at my wife, I feel regret, but I can't say anything because I'm too afraid no one else would want me. I know I settled."

"I can't tell my girlfriend that I settled for her and that I feel nothing, but I'm afraid to be alone."

"I've finally come to realize that I'm a settler. I've settled for my wife, instead of being alone. I've settled for the house we live in because it's what she wants and I'm just here along for the ride…"

"I was scared no one would love me, so I settled with my wife. I must admit I am now so miserable."

Loneliness is more detrimental to men than women and, as a result, they will go to any lengths to avoid it.

I remember a Katt Williams joke he had during his early tenure. He said, "The single life is all fun and games until you get home in that lonely kitchen." The crowd responded in agreement.

Martin Lawrence had an episode on his hit show, "Martin" referencing. "The Lonely Man" when Gina left him. He had one T.V. dinner in the freezer, "Lonely Man" Dinner. A play on Hungry Man. In television and film, when loneliness is referenced, It is almost entirely centered around the male. Living Single was a show centered around Happy women and their sisterhood bonds. Golden Girls was the same. Singleness and loneliness is a death sentence to males but not women.

The Manosphere and its subgroups, red pill and MGTOW, have made it worse for the average male. They have put the male aggression, entitlement and narcissism on display for women to see and have thus created a response in women to further withdraw from dating them. This has created an effect of a rising tide of single lonely men.

In addition to Red Pill and MGTOW, a growing sector called, "Black Pill" where "Incels" also known as involuntary celibate males are growing increasingly angry and violent because of their inability to gain access to women.

"I know I ain't shit! I can't keep a woman. I don't even want to refer to these women as women, they are bitches! Soon people are going to go ER, Elliot Rodgers. I am not saying going out killing random women is right and I am not saying I am going to do it. But I know that's what is about to happen."

This quote comes from a guy in the Black Pill community who constantly makes videos in that sector. Women do not get violent or aggressive due to loneliness. Yet, males continue to project their own fears and anxieties of loneliness onto women, who are quite content with being alone and amongst their social groups.

I recently came across an attorney on TikTok who was informing women on how to protect her children's inheritance from the new wife in the case she dies first. He stated, "men, on average, are in a serious relationship or married within two years of the wife dying."

This is not the case for women. Women typically do not remarry or enter serious relationships again. They opt out and prefer living alone while maintaining social networks. According to Pew Research, 54% of divorced women never want to remarry. According to data from the National Center for Family & Marriage Research at Bowling Green State University, the remarriage rate is higher for men than women. The remarriage rate for men in 2019 was 31.5 per 1,000 men eligible for remarriage. The rate for women was significantly lower, at only. 19.4 per 1,000 women eligible for remarriage.

Scientific and mathematical evidence suggests women do not desire marriage and men do, contrary to the, "we don't want to marry you or marriage does not benefit men" claims of the Manosphere.

How do you determine If you are dealing with a male who is lonely?
1. He has no higher purpose. He has a lot of idle time and does nothing constructive.
2. If he only goes home and goes to work. Very little to no social life.
3. Complains and speaks red pill talking points.
4. He attempts to convince you that he is ok being alone or that men don't need women.

If you give him your number, he will call you very quickly. As a matter of fact, he will constantly call you. This is a strong sign of desperation and loneliness.

5. If a male is ready to marry you or confess his love to you in an extremely short period of time this is a red hot flag.

6. He spends large amounts of time on video games. This is a sign of social withdrawal.

7. If he ever says, "feed me, fuck me and leave me alone."

8. He is a SERIAL dater or has multiple marriages.

9. He is married but constantly cheating and refuses to divorce.

The lonely man is a dangerous man. This man is only getting with you to keep himself company. If he suffers from severe loneliness, there is a high chance of him thinking, "If I can't have you, No one can."

Breaking up and separating causes physical pain in males. To cope with this pain, many of them get physically violent and attack to relieve pain.

My advice: Do not date lonely males. The risk is far greater than any reward you could ever get out of it.

CHAPTER 4

THE DESTITUTE MAN

"Property is not the sacred right. When a rich man becomes poor it is a misfortune, it is not a moral evil. When a poor man becomes destitute, it is a moral evil, teeming with consequences and injurious to society and morality."

-John Dalberg-Acton-

The above quote is infallible. Material wealth does not produce internal happiness, fulfillment or wholeness. It has no bearings on the soul. If one loses external wealth, it's a bummer. In other words, He is what Raymond Reddington, of the show, "BlackList" said, "Illiquid." His mind and internal value is still abundant, however, he is temporarily blocked from liquid currency to fund his endeavors. That's what black people would call, "broke." Broke is not a bad thing as it is temporary. A male who is broke is still level within. There are many homeless males who are broke, yet joyful and content on the inside. Being broke does not create a moral evil or a negative energy that disrupts the fabric of LIFE. However, when a poor man who is already broke without the necessities to properly sustain his existence and he has no soul connection, this is what creates the moral evil that is detrimental to life. He has lost the concept of what is right and what is wrong. Males are not the same as women. They do not have an internal moral compass. They have to be trained like dogs to behave morally. However, women do have a natural compass. This will be explained in greater detail later in the book.

In the case of the destitute male, the moral evil we speak of is his tendency to recklessly impregnate multiple women.

The destitute man has absolutely nothing going for himself. He has no value in his existence and the only thing he can look toward to give himself some self esteem or importance is his ability to produce off spring.

Males at the base of their biological nature are wired to compete to pass their genes along. It is the most important thing to the male. When a male has become destitute, he has failed at operating as a human in society and thus sinks to the lowest of his biological nature which has no governor or control mechanisms.

The male ego/self identity is extremely weak and is in need of constant validation.

The male gets his validation from how much access to women he has.

On my YouTube show, I analyzed a CBS Special Report in 1986 which covered the deterioration of the Black Family and Welfare.

The male, Timmothy, being interviewed had six children whom he didn't care for or provide for.

The interviewer asked him why he kept creating children if he couldn't take care of them. His reply was, "Well, the children are somewhat like art work. If you don't have anything at least you can say, I created this and they may grow up to be a doctor or lawyer and I can say That's my boy."

I also have an episode that shows 16 males created 336 children. The first male of that episode created 22 by himself and told the news reporter, "the court knows I can't pay no child support. You can't blame a man for loving women. The shaw family line will live long."

An African man found on TikTok, recently posted a "joke" about how African documentaries look and sound. He titled it BBC Africa. In the reenactment skit, James is trying to take care of his 54 children. James expresses to the interviewer "I am poor, I have nothing apart from sperm." Always keep in mind, that jokes are only funny due to their relatability and the truth that rests in its construction.

The destitute male is the male who intentionally creates multiple children and single mothers to fulfill his ego needs. This is a moral corruption and danger to society.

How to determine if the male is destitute. First, you need to know the definition of destitute.

Destitute is an adjective defined as -without the basic necessities of life. Similar words: devoid, bereft, deprived, bankrupt.

A male who is morally bankrupt, devoid of spirit, bereft, emotionally and mentally deprived will behave in insidious ways that will bring himself, the woman and the society down to the ground.

How to determine if a male is destitute

1. He complains incessantly
2. He pushes too hard to present the nice guy appeal
3. Many times, not all the time, but many times he can't look you in the eyes.
4. He is unemployed or no stable employment (frequently changing jobs)
5. He does not place much effort into his appearance
6. He has multiple children by multiple women

7. He does not have a place of his own
8. He has no purpose or vision for himself
9. He is validated by his male peers and always mentions his children and their mothers in any capacity. This is an ego booster for him. Especially if he is speaking on her negatively
10. He lacks personal accountability
11. He is heavily focused on sex
12. He tries to convince you that he's not like other guys
13. He is very sensitive to criticism
14. He has a poor credit score
15. He places a high value on his physical appearance if he has nothing else going for himself.

My advice: Do not date a male who is down on his luck. He is already incapable of love, so, you can't get that out of him. Sex is a reward for males, you do not reward males for failure and do not bring children into an already corrupt world that you can not save them from. Learn to love and pour into yourself.

CHAPTER 5

THE VIRILITY VALIDATION MAN

"Actually our virility depends on the gaze and the control of women. Without women, we cannot do anything. I think it's a good thing."

-Ousmane Sembene-

The nature of a male is biologically wired to seek an opportunity to pass his genes along. That is the ULTIMATE goal of the male who is trapped on the lower echelon of Maslow's Hierarchy of Human needs. A MAN is a male who has developed himself and reached Self Actualization and his drive is not rooted in or based in sexual conquests.

He has a higher purpose that drives his behavior which incorporates self discipline, control, direction and will power. Theodore Roosevelt said, "We do not admire the man of timid peace. We admire the man who embodies victorious effort; the man who never wrongs his neighbor, who is prompt to help a friend, but who has those virile qualities necessary to win in the stern strife of actual life."

According to Oxford Dictionary, **V**irility (from the Latin *virilitas*, manhood or virility, derived from Latin *vir*, man) refers to any of a wide range of masculine characteristics viewed positively. Virile means "marked by strength or force".[2] Virility is commonly associated with vigour, health, sturdiness, and constitution, **especially in the fathering of children**. In this last sense, virility is to men as fertility is to women. *Virile* has become obsolete in referring to a "nubile" young woman, or "a maid that is Marriageable or ripe for a Husband, or Virill"

The virility validation man can have the same character flaws as the destitute male but this guy is driven by his uncertainty of whether or not he can produce off spring.

This guy uses women to test the strength of his sperm.

This male will typically be older in age. He will speak about having a family. He could potentially be hiding the fact he has children already who are grown or with whom he has no dealings.

Males place a heavy premium on their ability to impregnate women. Without this ability, males lose a sense of purpose and importance.

Hedy Lamarr, an actress who was dubbed "The Most Beautiful Woman in the World" said, "Men are most virile and most attractive between the ages of 35 and 55. Under 35 a man has too much to learn, and I don't have time to teach him."

According to *Seminars in Reproductive Endocrinology*. Volume, Number 3, August 1991. Sherman J. Silber, M.D.

"Sperm count declines with age, with men aged 50-80 years old, producing sperm at an average rate of 75% compared with men aged 20-50 years. Between the ages of 20-39 years of age, 90% of the seminiferous tubules contain mature sperm. In males

40-69 years of age, 50% of the seminiferous tubules contain mature sperm."

The American Fertility Society recommends an age limit for sperm donors of 50 years or less.

So, as you can see, one of the key differences between the destitute male and the virility validation male is the age difference. If women like Hedy Lamarr consider males under 35 to be a waste of time and the peak of his virility is between 35-55, you can see where the motivation is for a male OVER 50 to pursue women.

Unlike the destitute male, the virility validation male may not seek out to recklessly father multiple children but he will seek to use a woman for the purpose of testing the potency of his sperm.

This is dangerous given the fact these males are targeting younger women who may be naive.

This male may or may not have stable employment.

How do you identify The Virility Validation Man?

1. Age. In this day and time, males are being hospitalized in the stroke ward at 44 years old. They are experiencing Erectile Disfunction, ED, at these young ages also. 40+ is when you need to begin checking for virility signs.
2. He will begin to heavily speak on family and how he always wanted one. He may or may not have children. If he does, he either has no contact with them, they are adults or he is unaware he does have them.
3. He will target young women in their early to mid 20's
4. He will heavily push his job, career or money.
5. He will push the narrative that he is a mature guy looking to settle down.

My advice: You have to determine if this is what you want. He may or may not stick around but his intent is to knock you up not to love you. Don't have children unless you are sure you can take care of them on your own and you have your own support system.

CHAPTER 6

THE TAX SEASON MAN

"The hardest thing to understand in the world is income tax"

-Albert Einstein-

This man needs no introduction. If you have a job, chances are, you will be dealing with taxes in one way or another. As you are aware, there are many males who do not have employment. During tax season is when males heavily seek out women who have employment and are getting a tax refund. For many women, this means a large lump sum of money that the average male can not get his hands on legally.

This one is commonly known in the urban communities. These males approach women who have low self esteem or those who they see as easy targets. They typically deal with women who are heavier set. This works very well if he is well endowed and attractive. They have to have some appeal to the woman that allows him to finesse her out of her tax money. Typically, it's telling a woman all she wants to hear, sometimes giving her a gift or trojan horse that she buys into. Then he gives her mind blowing sex to cloud her judgement. Finally, begins to paint many fantasies about making more money with the lump sum of money.

I remember a Facebook video that went viral some years ago. The guy was secretly recording the woman he was dealing with. She had just got her tax money. He asked her for a couple hundred dollars and spoke a bunch of fairytale emotional game to her. Once she gave him the money, he walked away exclaiming, "stupid dumb ass bitch."

My Advice: Do not give males your money honey!

CHAPTER 7

THE HIGH VALUE TRICK

"Try not to become a man of success, but a man of value"

-Albert Einstein-

In 2020, internet relationship guru, Kevin Samuels, made his debut to the world with his World Star Hip Hip clip. In this clip, he explains to a black woman how she is not worthy enough to get the type of man she wants despite her being a 6 figure business owner, young and attractive. This clip caused Kevin Samuels to take off with massive growth in terms of his newly coined term, 'High Value Man.'

Kevin told women that High Value men are men who make over 6 figures and have sustained it for 5 years. These men do not want a woman over the age of 30 and dress size of 6. He also coined the phrase, "average at best." Kevin was on fire, to say the least, until his untimely death in 2022.

Kevin's overall message to women was that they were "average at best" and no High Value Man wants them. What Kevin is calling a High Value Man is actually a High Value Trick.

A trick is a guy who pays for sex or women because he is unable to get access to the type of women he is attracted to without paying. He is willing to pay any amount of money because sexual desire leads and directs his actions.

The High Value Trick is a guy who had troubles getting women in his younger years. Now that he is older and more established, he uses his external value to purchase or lease the kind of woman who would not look his way while broke.

Albert Einstein made it clear in his quote. There is a difference between success and value. Value is what you offer and give to the planet, society, and the world around you.

Success is what is acquired for selfish reasons and gains. Males are primarily concerned with what they can acquire for selfish purposes. They are not concerned with being of value to anyone but themselves. By this reasoning alone, Kevin's assertion of High Value Man is flawed as it solely speaks of being desired for selfish and sexual reasons.

A true High Value Man would be interested in a woman who is on the frequency of adding value to society, the planet and the world in the same way he is adding value. This is a high caliber mind.

The high value trick is not after a woman for love or admiration, he is after her as a trophy. He is seeking to use her as an accessory. He has a nice job, car, suit, nice house and nice watch, he needs a nice looking woman to match all of the other accessories.

This man is only going for 9's and 10's on the physical scale.

My Advice: Women should not devalue themselves because they do not measure up to a male's taste in accessories. You are a human being with thoughts, feelings, talents and purposes of your own. The accessory to the High Value Trick is no more valuable than the woman associated with The Tax Season Man. All men are using you, regardless of the need you provide.

CHAPTER 8

THE FAMILY MAN

"The strength of a man is in his character. A strong man is a great man of wisdom who understands, his top priority is to his family."

-Ellen J. Barrier-

The idea of family is cultivated by society. Women are sold on the idea that she needs family, and in order for her to have a family, she needs a man. This is far from accurate. Women have always had family, as children are almost always more connected with the maternal side of the family. Men, however, do not have connection to family unless he creates a family of his own. The male's ultimate biological drive is to move around and try to find bodies to shoot his DNA into. This is not the female nature. The female nature is to nurture life all around her— plant life, social life, animal life, creative life, business life etc. The nurturing of life is not limited to child rearing. Because of this nature, she is more stable, stationary and purposeful. The male, by biology, is likely to leave his childhood family and search for his own family. Again, this is not the case with women.

Even when the male does create a family, he is faced with the ever daunting task of sticking around and being responsible for his creation. This is not a task men actually want. They don't want it because biological nature encourages them to seek high numbers, procreate and leave.

Before and during World War II, society branded manhood as aggressive, independent, stoic and competitive. This was a brand rooted in the nature of males which did NOT include being a humanistic, compatible partner for women. Stoicism, in and of itself, is the act of enduring pain and hardship without expressing one's feelings about it or complaining.

According to Psychiatrist Sebastian Kramer, 'males are attempting something extra all throughout life.' Unlike girls, who have better literary skills and more explicit about their feelings, boys tend to "clam up" when their emotions are high, feel uncomfortable and not know how they feel. In addition to this impediment, the male has to deal with high levels of testosterone and a pervasive sex drive which makes it difficult for him to focus, stay still and controlled. The responsibility of carrying a family on a male's back is too much pressure due to the biologically wired in deficits. By nature, males are less capable than women in most areas of life. In the wild, most males fail at surviving. They fail at passing their genes along. They fail without female access.

This male reality explains why most religious teachings focus heavily on women staying put and lowering themselves to be in relationships with males. Girls are conditioned to believe virginity is a prize. Nature does not support virginity. However, males place a heavy premium on it. Why? Males need to chemically bind a woman to them which makes her less likely to leave him. Listen to the male podcasters and hear how much emphasis they place on "pair bonding" and virginity. The more partners she has, the less likely he can chemically manipulate her. If he can chemically manipulate her, she is more easily conditioned to sacrifice her peace, ambitions, personal desires, mind, physical and emotional self to 'keep the family together.' She will remain through all of his transgressions. This is done through chemical warfare, subconscious programming through music and philosophy. Virginity allows him to permanently mark his territory.

It is innately understood by males they can not stay put or be responsible without external force. Women have been lead to believe her job is to keep a man, when in reality it is the male's job to keep a woman. However, males have a difficult time doing this because of their nature. Therefore, they need to condition women to tolerate adultery, domestic violence, stress, financial insecurity, etc for the sake of the male who can't stay put or keep a woman. If this works, a male always has a place which to return. This dramatically increases his survival rate and provides him the reward of passing his gene around over and over and over again. It's a win-win situation for him. This would not be the case in a fully natural environment; he would perish and no one would save him.

Men innately know this, as it is the male's brain wiring. Women don't know this. The male is a dependent in this world left to figure life out on his own. So, unless he creates a family of his own, he is without one for most, if not, all of his life.

Family is an insurance policy for males, therefore, it is his intent to protect himself from loneliness and lack of health care.

This is proven through this episode on my show, The High Powered Podcast. Skip to the 1:05:00 time stamp to hear it for yourself. https://www.youtube.com/live/2wUP6vJ_Xs4?feature=share

On this episode, Phillip Scott, another YouTuber, told his male audience, that men are going into the nursing homes as early as 40 years old and they need to get a woman and family so they will have someone to take care of them when they get sick and old.

How to identify if you are a potential insurance policy for a male.

1. Check his health history. It is a red flag if he has NO record of regularly seeing his primary care physician. This will leave you to be his primary care provider and waste tons of energy trying to get him to take care of himself. If he won't care for himself when selfishness is his nature, why would he care for you?

2. If he does have record of going but has serious health concerns, you should avoid him like the plague

3. If he has no immediate family and he lives a solo life. This solo life can become a strain on a man and this may motivate him to create family.

BONUS: CHECK HIS PHILOSOPHICAL BELIEFS of family and women's place in it.

My Advice: Always remember, the intent of males is selfish and not selfless. You must always look out for your own best interests. So, if you want a family and decide to deal with a "family man," Always keep in mind that the male chooses women based on the need he wants her to fulfill. When his needs change, his woman changes. So protect your own self interests even with a "family man."

CHAPTER 9

THE EMOTIONALLY IMMATURE MAN

Emotional maturity occurs when we express our true feelings without need for reciprocation, validation, appreciation or trepidation. Our feelings become companions and not enemies.

-LA Askew-

If you have been on social media long enough, you will have seen several instances of males who have opted to end their lives publicly for the world to see. Not only ending their own lives but many times ending the lives of those near them. Behind these acts of suicide and/or murder is seething pain from let down expectations of emotional void fulfillment from a romantic partner.

Males are emotionally underdeveloped relative to their female counterparts. It is partly due to the notion that males are supposed to be all masculine. This idea causes them to further suppress any form of emotion and seek to women to be their emotional crutches and outlets. The suppression is something that is already naturally wired into them, however, the philosophical program of machismo exacerbates the effects. This causes males to believe their only access to emotion is through women.

Let's take the 2022 Case of Francoise Littlejohn, who murdered his three children ages 6, 4 and 3 years old. He murdered them because he was so emotionally deficient that he placed all of his energy in a transactional relationship with the mother of the three children. He heavily depended on her to return emotional energy. Unfortunately, she did not. She left him instead. He felt her leaving him and refusing to communicate with him, left him no other way or choice to get her attention. Instead of reaching out for professional help, he chose to end the lives of her children and his.

How about the case of Ja'Dee Turner? On December 15, 2022 in Houston, Texas her ex-boyfriend lured her uncle out of the house only to kill her and himself in her bedroom. She broke up with him 2 weeks prior and had only dated him for a year.

Kelvin Brown II, an ex-military colleague of mine whom I knew personally, murdered his ex girlfriend in 2014 when she broke up with him. He was emotionally dependent on her.

We can talk about instances like these over and over again.

These guys are not getting in relationships with women because they love them. They are getting in relationships with them because they are emotionally dependent on them.

One of the key ways to identify emotional dependency is clingy-ness. When it appears that you are the center of their focus, this is a sign that should not be overlooked.

Another sign of emotional dependency is making you aware of all that he has sacrificed and done for you while simultaneously complaining of your lack of appreciation and acknowledgment.

When a person, especially a male, is willing to gut himself out with the intention of receiving certain emotional behaviors from you, this is also a sign that should not be overlooked.

When they initially approach you, they can present themselves in a variety of ways, so, don't place too much value on the initial approach but instead pay very close attention to subconscious behavioral patterns.

What to look for:

-How much of a victim is he being? Does he ALWAYS speak about those who have done wrong to him? This is typically bait used to draw women in for an emotional rescue mission.

-Does he try to rush into a relationship or long term commitment once you've done something he perceives as nice and caring?

This is a sign of neediness and or desperation.

-Is he insecure and heavily depends on you speaking life into him? This is a sign of emotional immaturity and fragility

Does he believe the role of a woman is obligation to serve his needs?

All of these are signs of emotional dependency.

My advice: do not volunteer to be his therapist or savior. Males must do this work on their own. If the house next to your house explodes and your house is within close proximity, your house will be damaged in the process. You do not want to be a casualty to someone else's implosions. Maintain your distance.

CHAPTER 10

THE SEX DEPRIVED MAN

"But when you're deprived of it for a lengthy period then you value human companionship. But you have to survive and so you devise all kinds of mental exercises and it's amazing."

-Wole Soyinka-

In this crazy new millennium, the man who is getting the most notice is the incel, short for involuntary celibate. These are males who do not choose to be sexless but are sexless due to some undesirable traits or characteristics about themselves. This chapter is not about him. This chapter is about another near sexless male and that is the sex deprived male.

The sex deprived male is a guy who has a wife or girlfriend but has been constantly denied sex.

The sole intent for his approach is to find a sexual replacement. He has no intentions of uprooting home because many of his other needs are being fulfilled. He will not throw that away for sex alone.

In 2014, the internet went ablaze when a man sent a spreadsheet to his wife for every time she turned him down for sex along with all of her excuses. The court of public opinion deemed this a justifiable reason to commit adultery.

So, be prepared for a male to lie to you about his marital status or to be upfront with the fact you're just someone he wants to sleep with.

You can not convince this guy to divorce his wife for you and you can't convince him to be with you for more than just sex. Anything you do outside of sex is a free reward that he gets from both you and his wife. He will play the game to keep you in his pocket without having to be committed to you.

I recently stumbled across a woman's channel, "Just Pearly Things." She had a male on her show by the name of Anton

Daniels of the "Lapeef Network." He verbally stated, "Do you think men care about what women think, feel or want? We, as men, slot women based on what we need them for. I focus 100% on me and her job is to focus on me."

If his woman is not fully focusing on him, he will step out and slot a woman for the purpose of using her to do what his wife has slacked on doing. Here's the kicker. One person can not do everything. Familiarity breeds contempt. Therefore, due to his consistent access to her, she will inevitably fail to meet his ego needs. Males are always on the prowl for something new and exciting. A wife is not new and exciting. This means he will cheat on her because he needs an ego boost that she can not provide.

If he says he is NOT married, do your due diligence and ask questions. You need to remember the answers to the questions that you ask so you can see inconsistencies clearly. When you ask these questions, ask them at least a month apart. If you do not have good ability to recall information, you need write it down. When you see an inconsistency, do not question him or make him aware of it—simply take note.

Many of these guys

will lie so its best to ask a series of questions informally and in passing.

Questions:

What is his name? You need a real name here because you want to verify what he tells you. If you're going to take someone seriously, a basic people search is something you need to be looking to perform.

It is important to know the real name of someone you are dealing with because they will need to hide traces of their behaviors and actions when you try to search for them after the fact. After the fact of some bogus shit they did to you.

In my early 20's I had a guy from the Nation of Islam run a hustle on me. He went by an Islamic name, however, his government name was kept hidden. I was eventually able to get it out of him. However, he made his whereabouts very untraceable after taking advantage of my naïveté and running off with large sums of money. My gut feeling suggested I do research on the inconsistencies I heard when he was telling me things. This was in 2008 or 2009, so, social media was still in its infancy. MySpace was a thing and Green Dot cards were too.

He told me he lived in and resided in upstate New York but his area code registered as Cleveland, Ohio. This was a red flag, logically and intuitively. However, I did not take heed. I should have, given the fact it was accompanied by a gut feeling as well. I was still new to being in tune with my intuition.

Where does he work? Believe it or not, many males will lie about this. If a male claims to be highly professional, it is important for you to take note of his ability to spell. Of course that would mean you, too, need to know how to spell. A male who has extremely poor vocabulary, spelling, and grammar is a dead give away he is potentially lying about his employment.

I recall a time when I was semi-dating this 55 year old guy. I was 28 at the time. A guy he knew asked me out. The entire time he was sending me photos of him in an operating room at the hospital and him in scrubs. He also had a decent sports car. I asked him what did he do for work. He said he was a "baby doctor." Then, I took clear notice of his consistent misspellings of multiple words. Men are ego driven. If he was truly a "baby doctor," he would have used the appropriate terminology to make himself feel superior to me. Obstetrician is the appropriate term for that, however, he didn't know that.

Illiteracy, poor grammar and lost on the word for 'baby doctor' was a clear sign of deception at play. There is no way on God's green earth he could have attended anyone's college. On top of that, my gut feeling told me he was on game note. Trust your gut ladies. I met him at a restaurant that was not 'doctor caliber' and then we went to shoot pool. He tried to sneak a kiss on me with out my invitation or permission. I instantly pushed his face away and he got upset, stormed to his car and drove off.

So, what was that about? Simple. He and the guy I was semi-dating were friends. I was 28. The guy I was dating was either speaking about me in a negative light which gave his friend the impression he could try me. Or he spoke in a way that made this guy jealous and competitive. He felt if the 55 year old could "pull me" then he could certainly have a shot. Since he drove a decent sports car and could pretend to be more prestigious than the 55 year old, it was no challenge for him. It killed his ego for me to push his face away. Him driving off made no difference to me as I drove my own car.

The more questions you ask, the more opportunities you can have to discover inconsistencies and lies.

My advice: Beware of a male who tries to conceal information or keep you doing most of the talking. You take control of the conversation by being the one asking the questions. He will either be uncomfortable, lie, give you selective honesty or be legit. You have to discover which place he is coming from. Do not dismiss gut feelings and ask questions about their true identity.

Also, please improve upon your personal knowledge. Contrary to the claims of society, who has lost its zeal for life, education, etiquette and personal achievement, grammar is important. Spotting grammatical and spelling errors is an easy way to determine if a person is lying about his or her prestigious career and educational background. Please invest in yourself educationally and don't fall for being grammatically lazy in this microwave society.

CHAPTER 11

THE DOWN LOW MAN

"A man knows what he likes, so sex with some men is like sex with a mind reader, someone who knows exactly how you like it."
— J.L. King, <u>On the Down Low: A Journey into the Lives of 'Straight' Black Men Who Sleep with Men</u>

I've spent a lot of time, beginning in 2016, studying and researching the psychology of the down low male. I have spent countless hours watching their YouTube channels, Down Low Chronicles, reading their blogs, forums and triple xxx commentary. I even went as far to create a gay profile on a gay app for men to further educate myself.

What I found is shocking for the woman who is blind to reality. The Down Low male is skillful and very in tune with women enough to easily use them as decoys to cover up their alternative lifestyle.

There is a man by the name of Immanuel whom I used to follow. He ran an online blog site, dl confessions sequel dot com, for over ten years.

On this site, he documented his sexual escapades with married men who lived up and down the east coast. There was no shortage of married men willing to hook up with him right off of dating sites.

The thing about DL males is they heavily depend on women to cover their tracks. They typically like to carry the most beautiful women on their arm because it creates a lot of doubt in the eyes of the public who may suspect homosexuality.

These guys will marry, they will get a woman pregnant or simply date for appearances just to give the illusion of heterosexuality.

Below is a reddit post of a guy who admits to intentionally impregnating a girl for the sole purpose of proving he was not gay.

"I poked a hole in a condom and purposefully got a girl pregnant to prove I wasn't gay"

"This was the late 80s and I was 14/15 and things weren't a great time to be a gay teenager not that it excuses what I did. I was so afraid of being outed that I started a relationship with my then best friend's sister. My friends were constantly messing with me about not having slept with her and calling me gay. They were just joking but I took it so seriously that I convinced her to have sex and I poked a hole in the condom hoping to get her pregnant so that I'd have proof.

She did end up pregnant and when I found out the reality of what I did, it really hit me. She just thought the condom didn't work and I never told her I did it on purpose. She was forced to go to an alternative school and eventually dropped out to have the baby. Her and her family moved away with the baby and I never kept in contact with them. I've always felt like a piece of shit for ruining her life and abandoning my kid."

Here is another: "I am a gay man and I am in love with my wife"

"I met my wife when we were both in high school. We grew up in the south, so me being gay wasn't exactly an option at the time. We started dating because it was a good cover for me, and she had a thing for me. I've never had much of a sex drive. I used to assume it was the pent up gay, but knowing the terms now, I'm probably on the ace spectrum. I definitely like men, but even with the hottest guys I only ever wanted it once or twice a month.

     I came out about 15 years ago, just to her. She was heartbroken, but very accepting. She asked me to still "date" her until I found a boyfriend, and I agreed because I did really value her as a close friend. We both agreed we would keep living together because we were young and couldn't afford the rent otherwise, go out together with friends, the usual, but obviously would start actively seeing other people. I met a few guys, but none that I really wanted to hold down, and she was happy enough coming home to me after whatever escapades she got up to…"

The key here is the INTENT. You always

must ask what is the purpose behind a person's decisions and actions.

So, how do you determine if a male is undercover and using you as a decoy?

1. How physically attractive are you? You must be honest here because this is a factor. If you are extremely attractive around the 9/10 area, you are a prime target. This is not to say that only gay males approach you, what I am saying is, this is something you must factor in when assessing the whole possibility. Your beauty makes it unfathomable that any male who has you would be sleeping with men.

2. Nowadays, males are bisexual so this part can be a bit tricky. The reason is because gay males have a distinct attribute of NOT engaging in sex, avoiding sex and or never initiating it with you. However, bisexual males will still sleep with you and enjoy it without giving the indications a gay male would give. If you are a 9/10 and this guy is not sexually pursuing you, there is a strong chance he may be into men.

3. If you are NOT a 9/10, a male can still be using you as a decoy but most often it will be through marrying you. Common law marriage counts too. Being married also acts as a decoy to an undercover male. The public just does not believe a male who is married would be sleeping with men. Even though married men are constantly caught with men, the public does not initially see marriage as hiding gay males.

4. If he is a member of the COGIC church and he exhibits these other characteristics, this is a HIGH alert red flag. The COGIC church is FILLED with undercover gay males.

5. He spends an enormous amount of time around males and he prefers the company of males. I have read countless forums of males becoming attracted to their male friends with whom they spend lots of time and documenting frequently how relationships develop between them.

6. He is heavily misogynistic. This should raise your antennas because males bash women because they believe it makes them appear more straight. This has been

said by gay males and straight males. Straight males believe only gay males and "simps" support women and side with women. Straight males do supposedly do neither, according to them. Because of this, you should really pay close attention to hyper anti-woman talk.

A commenter, G. Trabaldo, on Facebook left this comment, "that's a stupid argument. Dissing women is what straight men do. Gay men have no reason to dislike women. Heck, gay men pander to women all the time."

So, in essence, what he is saying is men who support or agree with women do so for deceptive reasons. 1. He is only agreeing with her with the INTENT to get sex from her so in this sense, he is straight but a simp. In the eyes of the Manosphere only simps tell women what they want to hear for purpose of obtaining sex. They believe an 'alpha male' doesn't have to do that and still get sex. 2. The male is gay. He must be gay because the only reason to agree with a woman is to get sex so if you're not agreeing with her for sex, you must be gay.

So that brings us to the DL man who uses this mass thinking process to his advantage. Bash women so he can appear straight/heterosexual.

Currently there is a question going around, viral. It was initially asked by Andrew Tate. The question is, "would you choose to sleep with a transexual who is a 10 versus a natural born female who is a 1 on the attractiveness scale?" Guess what? Men are selecting to sleep with males in dresses if he looks better than a natural born female. I mean, men are visual creatures aren't they?

Women face great health risks from this behavior. There was a nurse who called my show and informed the audience that women patients are coming in the clinic with fecal matter inside of their throats because their male partners are penetrating anal cavities without their knowledge.

My advice: Seeing is believing and the truth will set you free. Life is about education and knowing not ignorance and believing. So, you need to see with your own eyes what males whom you may be physically attracted to are doing behind closed doors. See how they are communicating in "safe areas." This is the age of information and nothing is hidden. There is no reason you should be just believing on blind faith. Go to the gay side of

Porn Hub. Search things like Gay thugs or Masculine Mandingos. Don't fall for the illusion. Question his sexuality if he is heavily misogynistic.

CHAPTER 12

THE FELLATIO MAN

"Clinton lied. A man might forget where he parks or where he lives, but he never forgets oral sex, no matter how bad it is."
— **Barbara Bush**

Barbara Bush, girl, you ain't never lied lol. Like Jamie Foxx said on one of his stand-ups, (in his Bill Clinton voice) "I've never had sexual relations with that woman! Get up, don't waste that! This is the fucking Ovary Office!" LOL The Ovary office! Of course I found this insanely funny.

All jokes aside, though. Males are very very needy. They are not self sufficient and they can not self sustain. If you truly know and understand this, you would never be jealous of another woman because he is only using her to fulfill a need the same way he is using you. He does not love either of you. In this case, if you are a wife or girlfriend, you may have a fellatio man on your hands.

This is a male who has either a wife or girlfriend who does not give head. This is a secret wish and desire for many males.

According to this anonymous questionnaire asked to married men, the married men admitted to desiring oral sex. The question asked was, "What is your favorite sexual fantasy that your wife actually would do?"

The Newlywed man said, "Oral sex as part of each experience"

The Conflicted guy said, "I would be happy to receive oral sex every once in a while. She's given me like 5 "successful" blow jobs in 16 years.

The Restless Guy: My wife and I have never been "adventurous" in bed.

The point? Males want oral sex and if they don't get it they will seek out a woman, potentially you, and use you simply for fellatio.

Devin The Dude, a Houston, Texas Rapper, said in the lyrics of his song "In and Out"

"Now I admit, I didn't put my prick up ya gal, she saves her pussy for you, she's just my dick sucking pal.."

Alpha Male Strategies, a male centered YouTuber, made it clear on his women's age guide video that "you have to give a woman an impression that you want a relationship when you actually don't. Tell her if you suck and little longer and a little harder, then MAYBE a relationship is at the end of that rainbow."

If you are simply just a fellatio need, this is all you will get in relation with him and you will spend your wheels giving him all the extra things just so he can use your face, body, money and energy while you get nothing in return.

How do you know? Simple.

How insistent is he about fellatio? That will tell you who you are to him.

Is he married, single or dating?

How much energy and effort is he placing into being in your space?

Is the effort minimal?

Is he actively trying to date and court you? Fellatio is inexpensive. Dating you and courting you is too much of an investment for fellatio, so he won't be doing it.

Does he insist on Netflix and chilling or randomly meeting you?

My advice? Don't be used as a fellatio girl and don't jump through hoops trying to market yourself as a benefits package for him to use with the intent of being the main chick. There is NO VALUE in being the "main chick.' So please stop fighting other women for it when it is a position of slave labor. It's not a badge of honor in the wake of the Divine Feminine takeover.

CHAPTER 13

THE JAIL BIRD MAN

"What I learned in jail is that I can't change. I can't live a different lifestyle-this is it. This is the life that they gave me and this is the life that I made."
— **Tupac Shakur**

I know you have to know someone in jail. If you do not know someone personally who is in jail, you know someone who knows someone who is in jail. Through your own personal experiences or someone else's, you know that jail birds are desperate. Jail birds are desperate for human contact, commissary money, Ramen noodles, a place to stay when they get out, gang related protection, a pen pal, soap-on-rope, a girlfriend with low self esteem that will marry him with 20 years left on his sentence and conjugal visits.

Because they need so much, especially, a place to stay and conjugal visits, they will seek out vulnerable women to leech on to have all these needs met.

It's quite interesting to see because these inmates have built up a psychological proficiency when scouting out potential women. Many of the guys are physically attractive. The more physically attractive the more leverage they have on a vulnerable woman.

I have a cousin who can't seem to stay out of jail. He spent his whole 20's in prison. He got out in his late 20's only to go right back. Before he got out, he preyed on this girl who then became connected to the family. Now, my cousin is definitely not someone any woman should build a relationship with. However, she built one with him while he was in prison. She had a place to live, a decent job, and a very meek personality, a personality someone could easily get over on.

My cousin built a relationship with her while in prison because he could use her to get on his feet. Once he got what he wanted from her, he began cheating and left her. That was no surprise to me. I have not heard from him or spoken to him in years but he began sending me letters from prison trying to involve me in some fantasy truck driving hustle out of nowhere.

When he got out, he came to me needing clothes, underwear and toiletries. After purchasing the items for him, I never heard from him again until he went back to jail. It doesn't matter if you are family or a stranger, they will use all to their benefit.

I even had jail birds inbox me on Facebook trying to run a hustle on me. Why do inmates even have social media access to begin with?!

Anyway, his initial messages to me were unsent by him due to his embarrassment of his failed weak game. However, I will give the gist of the conversation due to me still having having my replies to those now unavailable messages. He reached out to tell me he was 34 years old to tell me that he knows he is the one for me. He has been locked up since he was 19 years old. He was trying to convince me he had the wisdom to lead me. He was attempting to convince me, while in prison, that I should not judge him for being in prison.

He was also trying to bring me into some pō-nigga-mous (broke and dusty form of polygamy) relationship he was having with a correctional officer.

Here is one of my replies: "we will not end up in a relationship. The's not what I'm looking for so I don't really care if you have a woman or not. I'm not getting into emotional entanglements, relationships or potential sexual relationships. You see what I have to offer any relationship but what do you have to offer me if you're a felon STILL in prison? So far, I can't see anything I can benefit from while conversing with you."

As a result of that reply, he sent 14 successive messages over a 3 day period that I did not respond to, of course those messages were unsent by him.

According to my reply that I finally made after 3 days, it is clear that he suggested that I allow him to take 70% of any money that I make in some fantasy partnership he wanted to build with me while in prison. He said it, because I told him to send ME some money through cash app since he had access to social media and a woman.

He sent 13 successive messages over another 3 day period with no reply. All of them, of course, have been unsent.

It became evident to me that he is connected to a long time associate of mine who is a Pimp. Oh my, such weak game.

Because I did not reply to his 13 messages after 3 days, he then tells me, he has 1 year left on his sentence and he was no longer interested in me and I missed out on something good. I told him "I hope you finish your sentence" and I left it at that. Then, he messages me again 10 days later.

Although he unsent the initial messages, I have the second half of the messages here.

Him: Can I ask you a question?

Me: No. You're no longer interested in me right? So what do you need to ask me a question for?

Him: Shut up! Just answer the question.

Me to Myself: (Hmm real aggressive to be behind bars needing me)

Him: I still respect your intelligence. I just don't like you tried to charge me a trick. But this is the question. Can I come to Texas and learn who you are for real in the future to borrow your experience, education, native ability, and knowledge to accumulate wealth?

Me to myself: (I thought women don't have value. I could swear companies pay salaries for this stuff but I could be wrong)

Me: Nigga, you got me fucked up! I don't allow niggas to talk to me any kind of way. Remember, you're in prison. You need to stick with that C.O. you're fucking and stop trying to play like I'm one of these desperate hoes out here cuz I ain't the one. Now, get the fuck out of my inbox with that dumb shit!

Him: "I don't think 'your' dumb or desperate. I can USE an intelligent woman that's all. And your cooperation would be nice. And take me telling you to shut up for love.

If this doesn't make it clear to you his intentions are unscrupulous, I don't know what will. He blatantly tells me he can use the valuable asscts I have, I need to stop making it so difficult for him to use me to build himself up and I need to perceive abuse for love. Women's lack of knowledge on love is very detrimental to her life and well-being. Love is the power card men use on women. If women learn what love actually is and that men are incapable of love, all of these games become clear. She can stop males dead in their tracks without guilt or worry that she missed out on what I know for a fact to be bullshit.

    Me: Listen, I don't write or talk to my family members who are in prison. I won't allow my cousin to come live with me or near me. I'm not the one. No! You can't.

    Him: Don't see prison. See my mind. See that I'm a father and my fatherly spirit to provide, protect and love is all I ask. Then accept I have a great plan that requires the cooperation of more than myself.

    If you can't see the pure game and cookie cutter hustle spoken by the majority of black males, you will never see it. Here, he wants you to ignore his reality and create a fantasy world for him to exist in that is supported by the illusion of God. He wants you to exist in fantasy while he sucks you dry in reality offering you nothing tangible. Provide, protect and love…all from within prison walls. Laughable.

Your free husbands and boyfriends run this same hustle on you everyday. You can't see it because you're emotionally attached and are having sex with them. Therefore, you're blind to it but you can see it clearly from a random dude in prison. Sex and emotion is what clouds your judgment with the males you believe you know.

Me: Not interested. You're in the wrong inbox. I don't do niggas in prison. Too many options in the outside world. I'm not desperate.

Him: Look bitch! It's not about being desperate got damn! Get it through your thick ass brain. It's about team work make the dream work. Coming together accomplishing a goal, and after that's done you have a friend for life because you never know when you may need to call on a friend. A friend that do what your other friend may not do. Good night lady.

You can clearly see he needs me and not the other way around and was frustrated because I put up too much resistance and was not easy for him. He let it be known that he wants to use me using the power card of "love" to get me to allow it. Then, after his goal is accomplished, I would have a 'friend for life' which is code for I won't need you anymore. He was so frustrated that he got verbally aggressive. What do you think he will do in person?

My advice: do not waste your time on a jail bird. You are full of so much value that you and the world can benefit from that you shouldn't allow people to take tangible rewards from you in exchange for fantasies and temporary feelings. Listen to the everyday male who has nothing going for himself and see for yourself if he sounds the exact same as this jail bird. Also, if every male is hollering these same lines, it becomes clear that you are taking a major gamble on investing into any of them because you can't determine if you are choosing to invest in one who will truly succeed and do right by you in the end. Based on The Game: 41 Shades of Men, The Pursuit to Subdue and Use You, 9.9 times out of 10 you will lose by opting to invest in this bullshit game spoken by the overwhelming majority of males. Invest in yourself and a sisterhood and you will go much further in life.

CHAPTER 14

THE STEP MOTHER MAN

"Family isn't defined only by last names or by blood; it's defined by commitment and by love."
— **Dave Willis.**

Being a parent is hard. I know because I am one. Many of you are also parents. With motherhood comes a load of responsibilities that women are most effective at handling. Why? It is because women are naturally more capable of handling more tasks, have more effective communication, nurturing and rearing abilities. This is confirmed by multiple studies on women's effectiveness in the work place. Research shows males and females accomplish about 66% of their work tasks. However, women are given 10% more labor to do than males. This indicates women work harder and more efficiently. Research also shows that married working women still do the majority of the household duties. Males are not so capable of doing the same and are easily burdened with the added responsibility of another person on top of themselves.

Men, typically do not want the responsibility that comes with caring for others. They are selfish by nature and biologically ill equipped for large amounts of responsibility with many moving parts.

As a result, males who have been left with the responsibility of taking care of their kids will most likely seek out women to greatly assist them or throw off the whole responsibility on to them. Most often the male's mother is seeing after his children. If not, he has found a woman to do so.

Let's take the story of Eman Moss who was sentenced to life in prison without the possibility of parole for the murder of his daughter, Emani Moss.

Eman was the sole custodial parent to Emani. Emani's mother was a drug addict which explains why Eman had sole custody.

Emani met Tiffany Moss, her father's soon to be wife, at a Christian church in 2007 and supposedly got along with her.

Eman began dating Tiffany and married her shortly after. He began leaving Emani with Tiffany who began abusing her at the age of six.

After extensive abuse, Emani, 10, suffered a fatality at the hands of Tiffany. Her father allowed the physical abuse and starvation to take place because of his codependency and lack of desire to be a full time father.

Eman married Tiffany for the sole purpose of making her Tiffany's step mother.

In this case, the mother killed the child, but in other cases the step mother is killed mentally, emotionally and spiritually by the burden of children not belonging to her.

Below is an anonymous post made by a Step Mother.

Her: Can you please post anonymously? I am currently fed up with my marriage. I have been with my spouse for 9 years and married for 3 years. I have been the sole provider for the majority of our relationship, raised his 3 other children. (I was without kids when we got together) who are now grown and had a total of 4 children together.

The straw that broke the camel's back was that he was assisting in getting hotel rooms for prostitutes for his friend. He was caught by a family friend not once, but TWICE doing this. He claims he has not cheated.

Now, that I want this divorce, I am getting little to no communication from him to get it done. I don't want this in court or for my children to suffer. He is reneging on the agreement that was made for our children (together) to be taken care of in case of his demise. I want an out of court child support agreement and he claims he needs "time." I really despise going to court for child support. I know he is dragging his feet in hopes I will just go through the divorce process and not follow through with any child support or compensation for my kids."

Women are wholly unaware of them being used for male survival. As a single woman with no children she took care of 3 children who were not hers before she married him 6 years later. The primary reason he was with her to begin with was her playing the step mother role.

Mothers take on the primary and bulk of the responsibility with children. Males have a hard time being parents without mothers or women support systems. If a male is actively dating as a single parent, the primary motivation most often is seeking a woman to help or take the full load of raising his child for him.

My advice: Do Not allow yourself to be used as a step mother. The more you are sexually involved with a male, the more likely you are to stoop down to allow him to feed on you. Preserve yourself sexually and do not continuously sex him. If you attach yourself emotionally to a "step mother man," understand he will most likely intend to get you pregnant. This will ensure that you are less likely to leave his children if he gives them sibling between you and him.

CHAPTER 15

THE STD MAN

"To reverse the STD epidemic, we should all learn to talk more openly about STDs- with our partners, parents, and providers."
— **Dr. Gail Bolan, Director of CDC/s Division of STD Prevention.**

Sex has been around for a long time. A very long time might I add. Sex is a natural part of life and no one should feel shame for something that is part of their biological makeup. For ages and centuries, the most risky part of sex was an unwanted pregnancy. That would leave one with 18 years of responsibility he or she didn't want. However, as time has progressed, sex has become a lot more risky due to the increase of sexually transmitted infections. There are infections that can be cured with antibiotics because they are bacterial infections and then you have those which are viral infections and remain with you for life. Therefore, in this day and age you have to be extra cautious and aware. Well, this poses a major major challenge. Why? Because it requires humans to be full time conscious beings. Why is that a problem? It's a problem because humans are not conscious beings. They are subconscious beings. Subconscious behaviors account for 90% of human actions. To operate on more than 10% of our brain faculties, it requires us to be consistently consciously aware and heavily self controlled. This is presents a heavy challenge because humans are subconsciously motivated creatures. In addition to subconscious motivations, men are driven very strongly by sex, power and ego fulfillment. He will risk everything there is to risk for the sole purpose of obtaining sex, power and ego fulfillment.

So, who is the STD man? This is the man who has been recklessly having sex, not caring about his own health and eventually got burned with an incurable, viral based STI. As a result of this diagnosis, out of revenge and self loathing, he seeks to infect as many women as he possibly can. I have said on several occasions, penis is a weapon. It is a weapon used to impregnate women in order to slow her down with children. If he is jealous of her, he will use it to infect her with diseases and confuse her emotionally in order to gain control. Rarely is sex ever used by a male to truly express love and connection with a woman.

So, begin to see penis as a weapon. In this case, this man will woo you and make you believe he is very different and exceptional for you. He will do all there is to bring down your guard to have you have sex with him without protection.

Let's take Karim "Tyson" Zakikhani, he intentionally infected his ex-girlfriend, Sherita Anderson, with HIV when he knew he had it. It came out that he infected 7 others before her.

Raheem Bodiford of Florida infected two women, Danny Perry II of Nashville, Tennessee infected several and Valentino Talluto infected more than 30 women.

If a man refuses to be tested and insists on pushing sex without a condom, you need to stand your square and make him get tested or not engage with him. Do not fall for the nice guy, career or good looks as these are all subterfuges used to bring your guard down. As Sherita Anderson put it, "your health is yours to protect. Your body is yours to protect, don't put that in the hands of someone else."

My advice: Stand your square. Do not convince yourself to give into his wishes of unprotected sex. Do not try to be the nice and submissive girl. Do not fall for any excuse he uses to sway your decision on protected sex. Demand testing or no sexual contact.

CHAPTER 16

THE EGO BOOST MAN

"You didn't love her. You just didn't want to be alone. Or maybe, she was just good for your ego. Or, or maybe she made you feel better about your miserable life, but you didn't love her. Because you don't destroy people you love."

- Grey's Anatomy-

If you've read my book, "The 5 Components of Love" and took my, "Love, Men and Manipulation Decoded" workshop, you'd see the validity in the quote made on Grey's Anatomy. I will iterate until the end of all time that men are incapable of love.

Men have extremely weak egos and they need them stroked quite a lot. So, whether or not you know it, males will approach you with the sole intent of stroking their egos and making themselves feel important. Some of them love to be chased and they love having the power of rejection.

I am sure you have been on dating sites. Most people have in this modern era. Many of the guys who are on the social sites are not there because they actually have intentions to meet people. They are literally there to get their egos boosted. They want to see how many hits they can get. How do I know? If you've ever wondered why you just get a series of text messages with no initiative to meet in person, it's mostly because he's just playing petty games to boost his ego.

I remember I was going to meet a guy who was quite attractive. He was the type that definitely felt he was God's gift to women. I literally met up with him near a stop light as we both were in our separate cars. He told me to follow him and meet him at a restaurant only to speed away in his Mustang to leave me in the dust. When he took off speeding, I instantly knew what the game was. I did not even attempt to follow him. He never actually had intentions to meet, he was just having fun playing around with women and his fast car. He then messaged me the very next day about meeting up. Wow, what a joke.

The ego, simply put, is your selected personal identity. People attach themselves to external things they use to define their individual selves. So, in essence, people become their cars, clothes, jobs, religions, political ideologies, etc. So for him, his personal identity was attached to his car and physique. So, he placed himself in situations and positions that would allow him to highlight the attributes he felt defined who he was at the time. People with low self esteem or a low estimation of one's ego, are the ones who seek validation from external sources. These sources can be close relatives, friends or complete strangers. In this social media era, complete strangers are a big portion of that source.

Since a man's highest aspiration is sex by way of women, the biggest ego boost is access to women's wombs, affections and attention. His very identity depends on his validation from women. So everything a male does is to get your womb, affection and or attention. In this case, it's simply just your attention and him being able to toy with your attention makes him feel valuable.

My advice: spot it, don't waste too much time and play back if you want.

CHAPTER 17

THE NARCISSIST MAN

"Narcissists burn your sanity, erode your self-esteem, and make you doubt your own judgments and perceptions."
                           - Invajy-

The majority of narcissists are men. There is a reason for that. It's called NPD, Narcissistic personality disorder. From 2005-2010 I went to college and majored in Biology with a concentration in Cell and Molecular Biology. What I learned in my entry level Biology class is that LIFE has 7 characteristics. In order for something to be classified as living, it must meet all 7 characteristics of life.

These seven are 1. It must respond to environmental stimuli. 2. Have Cells 3. Change and Grow 4. Reproduction. 5. Complex chemistry 6. Maintain Homeostasis and 7. Energy processing

Based on these seven characteristics, we have to conclude that males are living beings even though sometimes they act as if they aren't.

The most important part of this list for this chapter is the first characteristic, response to environmental stimuli. Why is this the most important? Because the natural and normal response to stimuli keeps everything in homeostasis. Most disorders are a result of a response to anti-natural stimuli. When a natural stimulus is introduced, the behavioral response is consistent with that of other living organismal responses which maintain balance in the environment and within the organism itself. When an anti-natural stimulus is introduced, the behavior of the organism takes an odd turn.

The word, NPD, says it in and of itself. Dis-order. Narcissistic personality DIS-ORDER is a result of the natural order of life being flipped on its head and placing the male, who has a weak ego, into a position that over inflates his ego. Nature created woman as man's natural governor. Women kept the male ego in check. The male recognized her as the superior and bowed to her as god. Therefore, he never questioned or felt threatened by her ability to "overachieve and out perform him." But, ever since God was re-cast as a male, males have had a difficult time accepting the superiority of women. Instead of worshipping her, following her and helping her maintain earth, he sought to conquer her and prove his dominance.

In this modern day and age, males are extremely fragile and sensitive to criticism. Today, he is threatened by a woman's achievements. He has a difficult time proving his dominance without handicap assistance from laws and brainwashing techniques to give him an unfair advantage over her. There was a time this was not the case. However, since the induction of patriarchal philosophy by the Caucasian male, males have become increasingly more mentally and emotionally fragile. On top of that, during WWII, the government made it a point to exacerbate male nature and connect it to his sense of manhood for their purposes. The war promoted male aggression and stoicism as major traits of manhood. Both aggression and stoicism are natural male deficiencies. I say deficiencies because they benefit him in the wild but debilitate him in a community and social setting. Males are not communal and social by nature. Because the war campaigns inflated this nature, it added insult to injury. It created an additional psychological burden on the male which made it hard for him to adjust to society when the world changed to operate more communally and socially. Today, the male is still having a hard time not associating his manhood with these characteristics that are unique to testosterone.

Humans are the cells of this living organism of earth. The earth is in peace, harmony and stability when it is in a state of homeostasis. The planet is out of that state right now.

There are 70 million more males than females in China and India as a result of the government's anti-natural policies that murdered millions of baby girls. This gender imbalance created a ripple effect of political, economical and social dysfunctions throughout the globe. This living organism, Planet Earth, is required to be in homeostasis for its optimal function of sustaining life within it. However, due to the over population of males on the planet, and humans in general, it is completely out of homeostasis. Thus, why it has become cancerous. The male is the cancer in this planetary body. It is his over inflated ego, obsession with power and selfish hoarding nature, allowed to run free due to patriarchal philosophy, that has wreaked havoc on the planet. Narcissistic personality is a disorder created as a result of the male adapting to this unnatural environment. This can not be rectified in the existing male or current environment. The artificial environment would have to revert back to a natural environment and the new offspring would have to adapt to the new environment to correct NPD.

NPD is a danger to women and others because these individuals seek specifically to feed their ego/self identity. This should now lead you to question what his self identity consists of. You must know and remember the male nature is what is inflated. This can not be stressed enough. Males have been conditioned to see masculine energy as the primary and superior energy in all of life. Part of this masculine energy consists of testosterone, a chemical which induces violence and aggression in males. This chemical is unique to males as it distinguishes them from women. Therefore, they place a heavy stock into this chemical.

Every effect this chemical has on a male makes him feel as a unique individual thus is highlighted as a characteristic of his manhood. A few of the effects are as follows: violence, aggression, high sex drive, lack of ability to be stable and still, and lack of communicative proficiency and reduced empathy.

So, many times when these males get with women, they are getting with them for the sole intent of using them as emotional punching bags to make themselves feel more superior. They enjoy making you cry, they enjoy any amount of energy you give them even if it is negative. They will intentionally seek out weaker women to feed their sense of superiority.

My advice: learn to love yourself, Love yourself and eliminate the NEED for a partner. Get the 5 Components of love book and workbook. Come to the virtual workshop: Love, Men and Manipulation Decoded. Here, you will learn that you have never loved, never been loved and never known love. You will then be shown love and how to pierce the veil of deception using actual love.

CHAPTER 18

THE 'I WANT YOUR' CHILD MAN

"Abuse is never deserved, it is an exploitation of innocence and physical disadvantage, which is perceived as an opportunity by the abuser."

— Lorraine Nilon, <u>Breaking Free From the Chains of Silence: A respectful exploration into the ramifications of Paedophilic abuse</u>

Males are predators and conquerors by nature. They are needy and codependent by nature. They are hunters, they are not providers or protectors. Women are providers and protectors by nature. Patriarchal philosophies have programmed women to not operate in their protective nature but to instead seek outside of themselves and look toward the hunter, conqueror and predator to protect them. They were taught to look toward the wolf who dawns himself in the female/sheep's clothing. What clothing is of the female in this context? The nice, tamed, controlled, protective and gentle persona.

    To be an effective predator, you must seek out vulnerabilities and weaknesses that make it easier to catch your prey.

    Pedophiles are predators and their choice of pleasure is children. Who would be best suited to offer up this source of pleasure? A single mother.

    This is not to say that 100% of males approaching you are approaching you for your children, but it is to say that if you are a single mother and are being pursued you should have this at the forefront of your mind.

    Males have consistently said they are visual creatures and are sexually aroused by their vision. They have also verbally announced their interest in youth. Males can be aroused by practically anything. A sandwich, tree branch, or chair leg. There is no control of erections for males, especially in their prime. Age of consent laws are only laws because males will act in their unrestricted and ungoverned nature without them. Child marriage is still a thing, Islamic religions promote prophet Mohammad marrying a 9 year old girl.

If age of consent was lowered, males would proudly and publicly parade around with young children as sex partners. So, until then, the sneaky predatory intentions have to remain concealed.

He will pretend to be very kind, giving and extra nice to your children. He will do a lot to earn your trust. All so he can bring your guard down. Once you trust him and bring your guard down he has free reign to do as he pleases.

Below is a 9 year old reddit post that has zero visibility under confessions:

"[Listen] Confessions of a pedophile.

.

"I am a pedophile who is exclusively attracted to boys but I know all pedophiles inside and out. I will tell you about pedophiles who are attracted to girls and those who are attracted to both girls and boys. Obviously, I will not tell you about pedos like me. I believe most men are sexually attracted to young girls (under 14). They will not admit it but they are. If you ever run across a male who wants to be around your daughters, they are probably a pedophile. For example, if you date a guy who is very open to the idea of being a part of your daughter's life then that should be a red flag. Unfortunately, most women are too fucking stupid and desperate to differentiate between a man wanting to be with her as opposed to her daughter. Usually, the pedophile will be the knight in shining armor which women fall for all the time. Women usually have a fit about that because they want to believe they are good enough but they are not.

    Also, I would never trust any teenage boy to be around a girl. I can tell you that the teenage boy will have sexual interest in her whether he wants to or not. Why? He hasn't had the chance to sort through his own sexuality. Look at your teenage sons' friends if you have a young daughter. You'd be surprise how many of them are friends with him just to be near her. Leave a pair of her underwear in the bathroom and it probably won't be there after his friends leave. Finally, there are pedos who love both boys and girls. Those are the most despicable pedos. Those are the ones who would fuck anything because they have no self-control. You find those douchebags trolling on Omegle. A good example of those guys are on, "To Catch a Predator." They are usually the ones who give off 'creepy' vibes. Also, there is a long-running inside joke amongst the pedophile community. It's about how moms of fat and ugly children are usually the ones who are most paranoid about their kids being molested but in reality, no pedophile would ever want to touch them. Feel free to ask me any questions about pedophilia. You can PM me too."

Here is a comment reply to this post:

"I think you're projecting a bit onto other males. I do think a significant portion of men are attracted to women under 14, but I'm not sure if I'd say "most". I don't think you have to worry about most teenage boys being around girls, because whether or not they are attracted to them, they know that taking action is wrong and illegal. And most teenagers, don't have sexual interest in prepubescent children."

Many pedophiles are in a state of arrested development. Males are not born with any value to society. They must construct value through purpose and self discipline. Many find that to be a very daunting task which pushes them into the arms of children— very similar to the behavior of Michael Jackson.

Here is another confession from reddit: I am a pedophile

.

"I've been attracted to children for a while. I'm a teenager (wont say how old) and ever since i was 12 I started liking kids ages up to 7 and 8 as I got older I started liking kids 5-12. I want to like people my age but I cant, and I think the reason I am like this is because my whole life I was rejected by people my age. Children are the only ones who I feel don't care about my opinions, attitude etc. Kids only want what they want and I saw that they don't judge me for the things I do, the people I see or the things I do and they don't care if I'm weird, they are almost always joyful and happy. I've never even kissed someone no less hug or handshake anyone besides my family. and it's hard living a life of isolation because your emotions have been twisted beyond repair."

As a woman, it is your responsibility to protect your children. You need to love yourself and stop seeking outside of yourself for something a male is looking for you to give him. If you don't, you will be doing your children a disservice by placing them in harms way.

My advice: Never have more children than you can handle on your own. Stay single and childless until you have a strong support system, money and network. Love yourself. Check out The 5 Components of Love book, workbook and course.

CHAPTER 19

THE GREEN CARD MAN

"I think that we should give visas-green cards, rather, to people who graduate with skills that we need. People around the world with accredited degrees in science and math get a green card taped to their diploma, come to the U.S. of A. We should make sure our legal system works.."

—*Matt Romney*—

This should be a rather short chapter because everyone should be familiar with this guy. The guy that speak a no English and according to Donald Trump lives in "a hell hole country" and who so desperately wants to get out. By any means, will they get to the Americas even if it means marrying you to do it. The best chick to marry is an old and elderly white woman who wants to feel young again. So, in exchange for his green card he has to give her a lil suga' suga'. I have seen this all too many times lol.

If you are a Martin Lawrence fan, on his hit 90's show, Martin, the land lord, Luis, needed a green card and arranged a fake marriage between he and Pam so he wouldn't get deported. You should already be on game with a foreigner. They are in your inboxes on FB and Instagram running the same email hustles on you about being Prince of Zamunda and sending you 20 million Zuma if you take their hand in marriage.

Here is a mother who reached out to an author at the New York Times seeking advice for her daughter. "My adult daughter met a nice young man. They went for a hike. He brought along a man from an Eastern European country here on a work visa. There was chemistry between my daughter and this man, and they started spending time together; the original guy immediately stepped aside. Fast-forward: After a particularly fun hike and dinner, the Eastern European said they should plan a backpacking trip. They appeared to be on the path toward love, and my daughter was very happy. The next day, he asked her to marry him so he could get a green card. She was stunned and hurt. He was artless in his response to her, and then he ghosted her. My daughter is licking her wounds and embarrassed to have fallen for this scam."

Love is a man's power card. They know they are incapable of it, they just need you to believe they are. As long as women continue believing in a romanticized version of love and they keep believing males are capable of it, they will fall victim to all of these games.

My advice: Make your money, charge him a fee for that marriage and green card. Tax him but just don't let the income tax guy come swindle you out of your coins.

CHAPTER 20

THE LET ME MAKE MY EX JEALOUS MAN

"Jealousy is a disease, love is a healthy condition. The immature mind often mistakes one for the other, or assumes that the greater the love, the greater the jealousy - in fact, they are almost incompatible; one emotion hardly leaves room for the other."

— **Robert A. Heinlein,** <u>Stranger in a Strange Land"</u>

If you have this book, there is strong chance you have heard me say, Men are INCAPABLE of Love. Males are territorial and being territorial is about ownership and possession. Love is neither ownership nor is it possession. Males also have weak and fragile egos/weak self identities. They depend heavily on outside influences to make them feel valuable and worthy. When their sense of ownership is dismantled and their identity is shattered, only in this state can jealousy exist, thrive and flourish.

Males also depend heavily on projection to protect their own egos. So, a woman who breaks up with a male effectively impacts him in several crumple zones. She dismantles his sense of ownership, thus showing her level of strength and will power. This will power and strength mirrors back to him the deficiencies within himself in regard to his own strength. She also has impacted his sense of importance. All of this triggers jealousy. By choosing herself, she has sent a subconscious message to him that she is of more importance than he. Males need to feel important because they are born in this world without a strong biological purpose. They don't have the necessary tools, personality, or character traits to move forth a purpose if they have one. This need to feel important will cause them to behave in any way to get that feeling.

A person's outer world is a reflection of

their inner world. So, if a person is wanting to make you feel jealous, it is because they are jealous themselves and want to make you feel the same feelings they feel.

When a woman breaks up with a male, he will seek to quickly replace her and make it publicly known who he is dating. The new woman, he will praise, spoil and do many public appearances. The entire reason is to make the ex jealous. I remember being in an altercation with a woman, who was the sister of the guy I was living with at the time. There was an altercation because her boyfriend used me as a tool to ignite jealousy within her. This was neither a male I was interested in nor dating. Nothing of the sort. I didn't even know the guy. The only thing I knew about the guy is he dated her.

One day I was standing alone in the park looking at my phone. The park was a couple of houses down from where she lived. The guy came up to me, stood next to me and asked me for directions to somewhere and then left. This took all of 3 minutes at the most. Later on that day, I got hit in the face out of nowhere. Who hit me? His girlfriend. She thought I was trying to talk to her bum boyfriend only to find out later he was using me as a tool to make her jealous.

When he approached me, he knew she was watching him. She knew I was standing alone. When she 'found out', she later apologized. Women have an unhealthy obsession with males who can not do much for them. Interestingly enough, there are several pieces of advice online that tell people how to make their exes jealous. In all of the advice given, the common piece of advice is to, "Be with someone else…" "Pose with people who would make your ex jealous and share them online."

    The use of other people to make someone jealous is key. As a woman, you should never allow someone to use you as a tool to terrorize another woman. The only way you would allow something like that to take place is your need to feel important and validated. With that, you should do some self work.

My advice: Do not volunteer to be a weapon used in the destruction of another woman. Don't feel superior because he gasses you up to do it. She is not your enemy. He is the enemy to himself, her and you.

CHAPTER 21

THE PIMP

"Women say they want a man who knows a woman's worth. That's a pimp."

— Rich Hall —

The entire pimp game is based on seeking out women to use for all the internal value they possess. The use? For the Pimp's own personal gain, whatever he sees fit. You will hear people saying all the time, "You never see an old hoe but there will always be old pimps." Why? Because men literally suck the life out of a woman. The longer a woman is connected to a male, the more life force energy she loses. Males are attracted to life force energy. This is why they want them young. Years on the track sucks that life out of her. The pimp is a master at this direct energy transfer. This is who the average black male aspires to be.

The pimp is not interested in having sex with a woman. As a matter of fact, the pimp is the most disciplined of males. He is highly effective at controlling his sex drive. The intent and purpose of the pimp is to get women to provide him with a lifestyle of leisure via the use of her sex, money, youth and beauty. The pimp specializes in psychological manipulation to get a woman to voluntarily drain her own life force energy and freely hand it over to the depleted male. A pimp ain't a pimp without hoes. The pimp does not provide a hoe with a return on investment.

When you hear an average male claim he is not a simp or you hear him accuse another male of being a simp, what he is essentially doing is showing you he looks up to the pimp. A simp is the exact opposite of the pimp. A Sucker Impersonating a Mack or a PIMP. This means they have every intention on doing to you in a relationship what the pimp does to the hoe, drain you of your value. The pimp is looking for you to invest in him. Once you invest in him he feels he has power to bend you to give him more and more. You will know you are encroaching on the game when he tries to get you to give him something, loan him money, buy him a gift, let him borrow your car etc. These are all forms of investment that lets him know you have bought into him. I know a lot about pimps because I had two associates who were pimps. One of them I am still cool with. The other I completely disassociated with. Why? Because he used my friendship as a way to play chess and flank me from an unexpected angle. He did not try to cross me like he would cross a hoe on the blade. He wasn't asking me for a choosing fee or anything. He posed as a friend for 5 long years with a motive in mind for how he wanted to use me. Yes, he was an avid chess player who won many championships since he was in elementary school. He tried to set me up to take a large sum of money from me on the idea of business and partnership that was not centered around or inclusive of sex. It was centered around Podcasting. Needless to say, you see I am a solo podcaster.

    I remember, before I chose to start the High Powered Podcast, I was going to buy my own Semi Truck since I was in the trucking industry for 6 years. I mct the last guy I dated who was a millionaire who owned trucks. He was the actual straw that broke the camel's back. Anyway, I would get some trucking game from him and start my own thing. I started the LLC and all. I had the paperwork sitting on my counter and my Pimp "friend" saw the paperwork and asked where his name was on it. "I'm supposed to be half the owner of this company. You need to put my name on here," he says. "Excuse me," I say. He didn't even drive trucks or have anything to do with the trucking industry. Yet, he felt that any business I would do, I was supposed to have him as 49% owner. Yes, I caught on to his game quickly once he began to show blatant signs of a set up.

    Pimping is about using women to put money in your pocket. She doesn't have to use sex to get the money. She just has to see the male as the person to give all of her money to from whatever endeavor she is into. To make a long story short, I caught on to his game just before he was able to successfully set me up and I severed ties with him. Of course, this completely infuriated him. I didn't care because at this point, life had made me a master of male psychology and he was next to the final straw of dealing with males. Many pimps have High Machiavellian personality traits. I will speak more on these personalities later in the book.

Much of this game has been given in Iceberg slim's, PIMP and Pimping Ken 48 Laws of the Game: Pimpology.

My advice: do not give males anything at all.

CHAPTER 22

THE BUSINESS MAN

"Women will never be as successful as men because they have no wives to advise them"

— **Dick Van Dyke**—

If you listen to any male who praises a woman, you will hear how he needs her for him to be successful. He speaks on his need to tap into her energy so that he may have success and direction. He speaks of needing her to speak life into him and be his inspiration for accomplishment. He is practically incapable of accomplishing anything without a woman. The business man knows he needs the woman and he seeks to use her specifically for his personal elevation. He needs you to support him in every way and give your energy and presence to his cause. This can be risky if you do not firmly plant your feet into this work. Many times these guys don't have an income to take them where they want to go. They need seed money. They will get you to work and put them through law school, med School or fund their businesses. Once he's accomplished that, he trades you in for someone more sexually and mysteriously desirable to him. This is a high risk gamble. Marrying him does not ensure risk free investment. You need to be sure that you deal with this man as a business deal and not a marriage based on a shallow idea of love or you just selflessly "helping" your boyfriend.

    There is a woman, an attorney on TikTok, who gave women a public service warning about trusting their husbands. Her husband was a business man and was into real estate. Over the course of their 25 year marriage, they purchased properties together, or so she thought, until she found out during their divorce that she owned nothing and would get half of nothing, why? Because for the entire 25 year marriage, her husband was setting her up. He played on that fact and used the advantage of love and marriage to gain his wife's blind trust. He would show her a house and tell her they were getting it for their portfolio and she trusted him because they were married. He would then always catch her while she was busy and have her sign a bunch of papers. What she did not realize is he was having her sign papers that transferred all ownership to him as an individual so when he was ready to divorce her, she didn't get any of the properties. They obtained over 50 properties during the course of the 25 years. He needed her to build himself.

These types of males have a Dark Psychology personality type often referred to as, Machiavellian. This is named after Italian Diplomat, Niccolo Machiavelli. Machiavelli detailed the slick and ruthless ways of obtaining and keeping money, power and status. One of the traits of a Machiavellian is patience for long periods of waiting time. The machiavellian will make a plan and work it for as long as he needs to get the desired end result. Here in the example above he played a patient 25 year game on his wife.

Napoleon Hill, author of Think and Grow Rich, made it clear that scientific evidence shows the most successful men are influenced by women.

Men have to tap into the power of a

woman to catapult themselves to a high degree of success.

You will know who this guy is if he has a legitimate idea and is heavily focused on the need for a woman to do business. It is the woman that he needs help and support from, but in many cases they do not want to give you anything for your labor. They are selfish by nature so when you are dealing with them, you need to make sure you put your trust in legalities and not in him.

I found the following post on Facebook that was a short conversation between a woman and a wealthy and successful business man.

Her: "I asked a billionaire how he did it."

He said: "Forget about the girls and focus on one woman, she will help you achieve everything."

The intention is not to build a strong, happy or loving relationship with another human being; it is to use you to fulfill their self interests.

My advice: Do not go into a relationship with a man focusing on emotional highs and lows. Position yourself to reap the financial benefits of your labor. Your time, energy and help is not free. Don't let him guilt trip you into believing it is.

CHAPTER 23

THE POLITICAL MAN

"Politics is the art of looking for trouble, finding it everywhere, diagnosing it incorrectly and applying the wrong remedies."

— **Groucho Marx**

This man is very much like the business man except his area is politics.

Marriage is an unwritten rule for high ranking political officials. For example, there hasn't been an unmarried president since 1884. For 130 years all presidents have been married. Marriage creates the image of stability, maturity and responsibility. This image holds heavy in the mind the GOP as well as its voters.

I ran across an article written by a politician's girlfriend, Chloe Angyal. She states she is a member of the LegisLative League, an organization in Iowa that is designed for the political wives of that region. She proclaims to have been the youngest member and the only member who was not yet married to the politician she was with. In the article she specifically states the requirement of the political wife. I quote, "Political wifey requires doing the things that have long been expected of women: that they shelve their own ambitions in the service of someone else's. They show up, shore up, shut up and Smile"

She goes on further to say, "The political wife might also be the most influential advisor his or her partner has. And soft power- the ability to humanize a candidate, or help them network and build goodwill with voters and fellow politicians- is real power."

Michelle Obama was recorded recently professing to having given up her life to be a foundation for Barak.

My Advice: If a man is in politics and wants you to be his long term partner, the reality is he needs you to be the foundation of his political front and you serve a purpose to push forth his goals and his goals only.

Position yourself to get your goals accomplished. Investing is something that will benefit you.

CHAPTER 24

THE B.A.H. MAN

"The money game is not like any other game. You cannot choose whether you'll play, for the money game is the only game in town."

—Venita VanCaspel

So, you decide you want to become a soldier. You pack up your bags and head to basic training. You pass boot camp and are now an enlisted soldier. It was terrible spending 3 months in a bay with 60 other people, only to now be relegated to the barracks after enlistment to your permanent duty station.

You're also not getting paid that much but you do get a hot and a cot. You walk around base and see other higher ranking people getting paid more and being able to live off base. You would love to do the same but you're just a buck private. What in the world would be the solution to such an undesirable circumstance? Ha! Get married!! Why is that the solution? Well, it's simple, if you have a family, you can't stay in the barracks because your family will most likely be with you at your permanent duty station. So, as a result of having a wife, you will qualify for Basic Allowance for Housing, B.A.H. As a married soldier, the military will pay you extra to live off base or post. This is a strong incentive for a guy who wants extra money and to live off Base.

This pay is also increased if you're stationed overseas or to a combat zone. All of your pay increases. Isn't this a wonderful incentive to tie the knot?

Many military people up and get married solely for these benefits and they do not have any other attachment to each other besides this. Most likely, this will be done between military soldiers but could also be done between a soldier and a civilian. The civilian will not likely know this is his chief motivation.

I knew several soldiers in the military who pulled this. A close friend of mine is one of them. He and his significant other married solely for the extra money. They didn't even talk. They did their own thing and when the significant other fell short, a divorce and alimony stunt was pulled. The spouse eventually committed suicide due to the inability to deal with life.

Another friend of mine, a soldier, married another soldier. They got the same benefits, however, their relationship was riddled in problems. She called me back in 2014 and I gave her wisdom she wasn't ready to hear at the time. She was in a relationship all by herself. Needless to say, they finally divorced around 2021 after she began to embody the reality. Please believe he put her through hell. He tried to destroy her credit, brought another woman into the house, brought terror to the children and all. He did it simply because she took the power and left him.

My advice: If you marry a military man, understand he is getting paid extra to have you as a wife. He gets monetary incentives from the organization, slave benefits from the wife, sexual release and the ability to still get sex behind her back. All of this at the expense of the woman. Make sure you set yourself up to win and do not believe for one second love has anything to do with this.

CHAPTER 25

THE MURDER MAN

"The first time I killed somebody, it was such a rush, it was just like that, a shot of dope every time I did it."

—Tommy Lynn Sells

His mother treated him horribly, abandoned him, starved him of affection and neglected him for what he felt was of least importance to him. She had dark hair, light complexion, 5'6" and slender. He has always wanted to get revenge on such a woman. Interestingly enough, you look just like her. As a matter of fact you have a striking similarity that triggers these feelings of revenge.

He is a throw away to society and no one really cares about him and he's an easy target. He was picked on. No girl or woman has ever shown interest in him. He is a reject, a shelved artist with a disappointed existence. Here you come, a triggered image of revenge.

These males are psychopaths and are not approaching you at all because they like you or want to love you. They have a desire to inflict pain on you or to perhaps, take your life away from you. Jealousy, rage, envy or just a sick perversion creates this desire in them to pursue you. Every man isn't coming to you because he's attracted to you and just wants to spoil you. He's approaching you because he wants something from you or to do something to you which, in turn, gives him a feeling of euphoria or vindication.

Let's take serial killer Samuel Little. He confessed to killing 93 people, nearly all women between 1970 and 2005. He had a distinctive profile of a woman he pursued all with the intent of killing them. Of course, the victims were unaware of his intentions. He pursued women who society wouldn't miss and who led night lives. He enjoyed strangling them.

Andrew Tate, former professional kickboxer, was caught telling a woman that he enjoyed raping her. The more she fought back and denied him the more it turned him on. There was a post that went viral in 2015 where males were telling women to just lay there and let a man rape them if they got raped. Women were noticeably upset because of this. However, what they didn't realize is the males were telling them that the act of fighting back increased the excitement within them. Playing dead was what the cartoon characters used to do to deter wild animals. There is a scene in the movie "Ice Age," where the animals saw a preying hawk flying above them and they instantly played dead to deter the hawk from attacking them. This is the exact same strategy the males were suggesting women pull on men who would proceed to rape them. If she doesn't fight back, the male will not get the thrill and excitement of obtaining power over her by physically overpowering her.

    Ted Bundy had an obsession with killing college women. He lured the women with a vulnerable approach. He enjoyed raping and strangling them.

    John Norman Collins, suspected of killing 8 or more women, had a pronounced revulsion for menstruating women. Several of the women he killed were on their cycles at the time he killed them.

Edmund Kemper enjoyed preying on hitch hiking women. At age 15 he murdered his grandmother. It is reported he murdered at least 6 coed females and beheading them.

Marc Lepine- The man who hated women, killed 14 women and smiled throughout each attack. It is said that he grew up "nursing severe grudges against women and feminism, in particular." It is said that he called a group of males and females into a classroom and separated them into two groups. He told the group of males to leave and killed 6 of the 9 women who remained by gunshot. He left a suicide note listing all the political women he wanted to murder before he died. He blamed women for his life failures and his insignificance to society.

This last example is definitely something of which to take notice. As radical male podcasts and the growing pool of single lonely males continue to rise, the conversation regarding women's safety becomes more center stage. Matricide, infanticide and femicide rates are rapidly increasing as these social structures continue to collapse. The males are angry, disenfranchised and lost. People like Kevin

Samuels and Andrew Tate only encourage behaviors such as these to persist.

My advice: Be very careful with just assuming a male is approaching because he thinks you're attractive. Learn to quiet your mind and tune into your intuition. Use The 5 Components of Love to pierce the veil of deception and heighten your intuition.

CHAPTER 26

THE FETISH MAN

"Fetish is the exploration of sex as art, and the refinement of one's personal desires. Anything can be fetishized...There'll be new fetishes forever. I feel that the 21st century is all about fetish."

— **Rick Castro**

Humans are interesting creatures. We don't realize we are because the artificial, socially constructed population has relegated human nature into the shadows. However, since the new days of the internet, it's much easier to find the shadows of human nature. All you have to do is locate a forum and voila! The shadow. For a long time humans have tried to force sexuality into a black and white box. Black and white are the only absolute colors on the spectrum. There are no other absolutes. Sexuality is one of those things that is not absolute. Attempting to box it into an absolute has never worked. However, the powers that be, through the control of media and media outlets, led the populace to believe otherwise.

In the shadows, people can really be who they are without public ridicule. In the underground, people can also find exactly the type of person they need to fulfill these sexual fetishes. In the underground you will discover websites you had no clue existed.

The fetishes can be great and many. They may range from toe licking to passing gas in a jar and selling it. That sounds crazy, I know. However, I promise, there is a lady on TikTok who is currently being paid thousands of dollars to perform sexual fantasies for males. One of her clients is a high ranking military officer who likes her to pass gas in a mason jar and send it to him. I believe she said he paid her $700 for it. Listen, some of these ladies are really taxing the guys.

There are guys who like to feed obese chicks and eating the booty like groceries. Whatever the case, the fetish guy is using you for a fetish.

This is obvious in this case, however, there are average everyday, regular dudes who approach women because they see them as fetishes. They want them as fetishes but don't have fetish money. So, they get in relationships with them. They are getting in the relationship because they can not afford to just pay her for the fetish and they may also need her for an ego boost and a place to stay. So, this is potentially a triple threat intention. Therefore, for him, it's best to get in a relationship because relationship means 'FREE access' to all of these needs and wants.

How To know if he fetishizes you.

1. He obsessively speaks about an odd trait about you. If you pay very close attention to his subconscious speaking patterns, it will be the first thing he mentions and something he mentions quite frequently at different times in the future.

2. He expresses constant sexual fantasies that include "your type"

3. Obsessively preoccupied with thoughts of your type. You can observe this is his

speech or preferences he brings attention to on his social media posts.

My advice: Always remember as a woman, you are a resource. You are providing and servicing a need.Do not deal with this male unless you know exactly what you are getting in return and make it worth your while.

CHAPTER 27

THE PRO BLACK HOTEP MAN

"We was Kangs…"

— **Every delusional participant in this sector**

Since before the civil rights movement of 1964, black people had come up with ways to feel good about themselves and their identity. This was motivated by the destructive philosophy of racism and politics. During this time, The Nation of Islam made its mark with figure heads like Malcom X and Muhammad Ali. The Black Christian Church also had its figure with Martin Luther King Jr. The Civil Right's movement made a lane for the prevalence of the consciousness movement that would proceed to dominate in the 80's and early 90's. Moving into the

70's after the civil rights movement, is when the steam began to build up.

There was the Black Panther Party, afros, and James Brown with I'm black and I'm proud. This image and movement was needed during the time of Jim Crow, redlining, and the projects. These political policies made life even more difficult for blacks because the environment was harsh and artificial. White America was not knowledgeable about the effects environment has on a living organism. They didn't think deeply. They just followed along with the psychological programming of superiority they've been indoctrinated with for centuries. White people voted for political policies against black people that were rooted in their psychological programming which created the artificial environment black people lived in. As a result, Black people had a bad look on them because of these racist policies which acted as a stimulus in creating a negative response in their behavioral patterns. These historical atrocities left Black people with severely fragmented egos. Ego development is important for personal development before one can overcome the self.

Moving forward into this new age of

identity for black people, spawned even more sectors for this identity confusion. The sectors include but are not limited to ancient Moors, Muslims, Hebrew Israelites, Sabians, Kemets, 5 percenters, Nuwapian Nation, Pan Africanists and most recently added to the list is Carbonation.

These different sectors of identity fall within the dynamic of the love and belonging region in Maslow's Hierarchy of human needs. Remember, this is a lower nature deficiency need. The male's ego is in constant need of boosting and protection. Identity is severely important to him. Therefore, all of these sectors, too, are rooted in patriarchal philosophy which means they are male dominated and centered.

As a result of the psychological abuse endured by black people, as a whole, alongside male nature, black males hijacked the movement and focused on the advancement of the black male. This largely excluded women's plight and contribution. The motivation for a Pro Black male was to get women to uphold the illusion of the strong black male image. It promotes success for the male ego to be seen in a light of strength when in actuality he sees himself as defeated. He needs a woman who is a willing participant to sacrifice herself to uphold the illusion. Back in the 90's Shaharazad Ali produced her book, "The Black Man's Guide to Understanding the Black Woman." This book detailed how to use black women to salvage his image and ego. She recorded a home made video with a poem/rap song at the beginning. Here are the words to this poem.

"Look at me, I'm the black man. Me and my woman are lost, traveling in a strange land. I'm having it hard and my future looks bland. And No, I don't expect you to understand. I', doing bad for all to see. But all this universe belongs to me. And I plan to get on the right track as soon as I get my woman back."

This poem says two things: 1. The woman is the reason he is unsuccessful. 2. He needs the woman to use as a stepping stool to not be doing so badly. If this is the case, which it is, exactly what does the woman need him for? She can do bad by herself. His bad habits that cause him to be a failure will only be carried over into the relationship which will burden women even more. Have you experienced having more burden with a man present and less burden when he's absent? If so, this is why. Patriarchy is an artificial system. It is a wheelchair ramp for males. White men created this wheel chair ramp for themselves and largely left black males out of it. Black males felt this lack of privilege and decided to use black women as stepping stools to boost himself in comparison to the white male. The Pro Black philosophy is riddled with males who are struggling with their own natures. They are not biologically wired to lead or carry large amounts of responsibility.

  The white man's "Boy's Club" created a network of opportunities they hoarded for themselves and passed down to their buddies. Most often their buddies were not qualified. It's to their saying, "Most deals are made on the golf course." It's not what you know, it's who you know. So, the boys didn't actually need skills, they needed connections — connections not afforded to black males. The major responsibilities of these networks were built on the shoulders of white women. White men needed white women to advance to the levels in which they've advanced. Outside of the business of slavery, white women are largely responsible for the successes of white males, even though they've been mostly overshadowed by them.

    Though white male patriarchal philosophy and structures did not pass social, political and economic power down to the black male, it still stroked and inflated his ego. He adopted the idea of men being the leaders and heads of household. He also adopted the idea of God being male. Because he attempted to emulate white males who overshadowed their women, he effectively destroyed his own power source, black women. The black male's original way was underneath the worship of the women—matriarchy and matrilineal structures in line with nature. He abandoned this way and began to adopt the ways of the white male without complete comprehension of the philosophies of white men. Without the wheel chair ramps of patriarchy created by white men for white men, and the power source of the black woman, the black male found himself isolated, disempowered and a complete victim of circumstance. Because of this, the Pro Black Movement became all about him. This male will guilt trip you and get you to buy into the idea of saving the "black community." He wants you to place him on a pedestal and be the wheel chair ramp white males won't let him use in a white male patriarchy.

My Advice: This era is dead. We are in a state of rising consciousness that is technology and female centered. It does not benefit you to carry racist, colorist, or sexist philosophies. Do Not volunteer to be his wheelchair ramp. Allow him to sink or swim. Either he makes it on his own or he fails. His failure is not your responsibility nor is it your fault.

CHAPTER 28

THE I'M BORED, WIFE NO FUN

"Familiarity Breeds Contempt."

— **African Proverb**

They say women are from Venus and men are from Mars. There may be a lot of truth to that given the fact mars once was a thriving planet of resources like earth and is now completely uninhabitable. Leave a male in your home for a week or two alone and you may come back to an uninhabitable place. Also, males have no comprehension of higher love frequencies. On top of that, masculine energy is a moving energy that needs to keep going. Because of that, males can easily bore. They can easily bore of routine and lack of activity. When the wife is not adventurous, she can become complacent and lack life force energy that inspires the male to move. When this happens, males will up and seek a thrill.

Typically, that thrill will be with another woman. There is nothing more exciting to a male than engaging in behavior that is taboo or secretive. This brings life back into his being. When a male is stagnant and not moving, he feels like the end is near or his mortality is catching up to him. So, it is necessary that he find something that reignites the flame within him. This is where you may be used as that flame. Sex is fun to men, it is not something they use to love a woman in the overwhelming majority of cases. Sex is fun because it triggers the reward system in their brains when they chase or play the game to get it.

There is also nothing more fun than being with a new person who takes an interest in who you are, your hobbies and interests. The wife has typically, grown too familiar, become bored, disinterested and too busy to take an interest in her husband the way she did at the beginning. Males are co dependent by nature and need constant attention and reassurance. They lack the ability to provide this for themselves.

Therefore, once you slack on this, he will desperately seek outside of himself to get this attention and reassurance.
This guy could tell you he's married or he could lie to you. You won't know unless you pay attention to how he moves. Most males will not be monogamous. If he has good looks, money and a decent personality there's a strong chance you are not the only one. If the majority of the time you two are having fun and there's not much weight placed on you, then chances are, you are someone he is having fun with but is not planning on uprooting his home life for.

It is not impossible you are the only one but it is highly unlikely.

Here is a confession I found on reddit:

My wife is boring and I think I will end up cheating on her.

"We've been married for 5 years now and sex has always been a problem. She never wants to try anything new. She's always tired. She's not in the mood. I'm the one working 40+ hours a week so that she can just stay home and watch the kids but yet I can't even get a BJ when I get home tired. I have to beg for a simple kiss. I can't even touch her unless she's in the mood which never happens. She doesn't want to go on dates because no one is good enough to watch the kids or why waste money or she's tired. Excuses after excuses.

We have kids between 2 and 5 so I get that she can be tired but every single day? Not trying to be selfish but how am I supposed to stay in love with someone I'm never intimate with? How am I supposed to be attracted to someone who doesn't even try to be attractive? How am I supposed to look at younger, more attractive women and not be tempted? How am I supposed to look at an opportunity to have sex, be intimate, have an exciting relationship and say no? **Side note:** (As you see, males despise responsibility and all that comes with it. There are no days off with children between the ages of 2 and 5. Not to mention, in addition to, an adult child)

I'm tired of not being able to talk to her about anything other than kids, money, and cleaning. I'm tired of having to watch porn and use my hands (if you see what I mean by that). I'm tired of this boring marriage and as much as I'm against cheating, I feel like that's my only chance at living something exciting without destroying my family. **Side Note:** (He, evidently, has much more time on his hands than she does. She works 24/7 and has no outside help. He lacks the understanding of this. No, you can't trust everyone with your children.) If you guys have any advice for me that'd be great.

Edit: I do help with household chores when I get home from work. A lot of times, I get in trouble because I don't clean the way she wants me to, don't put stuff where she wants them to go. I just never do anything right. So at times I give up on helping a little bit. But I always do some! So no, I'm not this selfish guy who doesn't care about how busy/tired his wife is and just wants sex. Also, I know being a stay at home wife is a lot of work. When I said "I'm the one working 40+ hours a week so that she can just stay home and watch the kids", I meant that I work extra so she doesn't have to work a regular job on top of taking care of the house and kids."

Monogamy is an unnatural set up. A nuclear family is also unnatural. These relationship and family dynamics place extreme pressure on both the male and female. It eliminates the support system and community that women have relied on since the beginning of time. It also isolates her and forces her to 1. Do all the work, designed for multiple women to do with each other, alone. 2. Look to the male, who is a natural co-dependent parasite, to help her. His predatory nature is to hunt, kill, hoard and leech, not carry responsibility. By forcing both parties to be in anti-natural set ups, it mentally breaks them both down and creates never ending relationship problems. Monogamy and a nuclear family does not support the nature of either party. The male does not have the brain capacity to handle large amounts of pressure and responsibility. He will ALWAYS seek women to do the mental, emotional and responsibility heavy lifting. Forcing square pegs into round holes is grounds for suicide, murder suicides, 'cheating,' and domestic violence.

     Monogamy was set up to cater to the needs of a male. In nature, the vast majority of males would not survive. Monogamy prolongs his existence because it gives him access to women he wouldn't have in the wild. Women protect males from loneliness, health disorders, lack of sex, and other normal male threats. However, by catering to his needs in this way, you also destroy him in the process. There is no perfect world for the male. He's damned in nature and damned in the matrix. He suffers in nature and he suffers in an artificial environment.

Since the average male and female are not the creators of patriarchy and the woman is largely ignorant of the male makeup, there is confusion and chaos created that "communication" won't fix. The communication will only continue to force both parties to go against their natures which is the problem to begin with.

The male is upset that she doesn't understand his need to be rewarded with sex and fun in exchange for him going to work. In nature, "going to work" is nonexistent for the reward of copulation. The male's idea of being rewarded with a woman's body for doing something beneficial to his own growth or slave labor to the ruling class is delusion. Working 40+ hours a week is a man made system. The woman's natural desire for sex is not triggered by a male slaving for a system. Jobs were handed down to males in the wheel chair ramp of patriarchy to pacify them. Women were stripped of their right to provide for themselves and forced to depend on males for fiat resources. She was sold a dream of being a sex and domestic slave for the male. The male adapted to this artificial environment and began to expect these results even though it goes against the nature of himself.

Women were communal and had matrilineal family ties which created a support network for her.

Women did not carry the burdens of all of the labors on her own. She also did not depend on males to help in these areas. These duties were shared amongst the community. Everyone pulled their own weight.

The nature of the woman is not to be continually penetrated regularly and the nature of the male is not to have access to abundant sexual opportunities unless he is biologically the fittest. Him being the fittest has nothing to do with going to work a 9-5 job given to him by an establishment.

Both parties in this situation are ignorant of these realities and they are desperately trying to live an inorganic artificial life they are both failing at.

The male will not go against his nature very long. If there is an opportunity for sex and fun, he will seek it outside of this union. Familiarity breeds contempt. Living together creates major problems for heterosexual couples. Seldom visit makes a longer friendship. Seldom visit maintains mystery and protects both parties from the dark side of human nature.

My advice: Stop trying to force monogamy and stop living with your partner if you are in a heterosexual set up. Men can live with each other and women can live with each other without major problems. However, men and women living together more often than not creates unbearable problems for both parties. He will "cheat". He will lie. He will sneak and he will fall short on critical obligations and duties. Re-establish your bonds between other women. Place yourself and your female relationship bonds above male needs. Also, do not allow the idea of marriage to cause you to lower your guard on safe sex. Males will step out and bring you something back. Stop concerning yourself with whether or not you're going to hurt his feelings. He is not going to think twice about hurting yours if he wants a paternity test, married or not.

CHAPTER 29

THE INSECURE SABOTAGE MAN

"I did bully someone. I was insecure."
— *Matt Lauria* —-

You are youthful, beautiful, career driven and accomplished. You are everything a male wants but knows he is too unachieved and unaccomplished to deserve. Yet, somehow he gets access to you. This male is not driven to you because he likes you, wants to marry you or establish any long term relationship with you. His entire objective is to conquer you and slow you down. He perceives you as a weaker vessel who believes you are better than him because of your accomplishments.

You dominate in everything from financial gain, career, sex appeal, and charisma. You reign over him in so many ways and he knows this. He knows he can't hold a candle to you, defeat or conquer you in any of those areas. He sees you really can do everything he can do better. However, he knows he can do one thing you can not do. He can effectively alter the entire course of your life with one action. He knows he can and wants to throw a monkey wrench into your plans.

Males believe that accomplishments and high financial achievements are areas for men to dominate and flourish. Therefore, if a woman is accomplishing and rising in this arena, she must be attempting to act like a man, take the place of a man or compete with a man. This makes his chief intention to show you that you can not do everything a man can do and you will not rise higher than himself. So, he effectively uses his penis as a weapon to slow down the trajectory of your life by giving you a baby to take care of. This is all ego behavior.

Many times the insecure sabotage man has no area in his life which he controls, dominates or feels important. Therefore, this guy will not ever move to help you take care of the child he intentionally gives you. He wants to establish an area in his life where he can have three of his critical needs met, Power, control and a sense of importance. If he gives you a child and abandons you and the child, more often than not, the woman will chase and beg him to do his part. This gives him a sense of power, control and a feeling of importance. He enjoys dodging you. He enjoys the frustration he is causing you. He gets the power he was lacking. His actions are the cause of your pain, his happiness and acknowledgement. It makes his ego feel so great when he can look at his friend and say, "She is just mad because I don't want to be with her in a relationship any longer." The person who has the ability to reject and deny has power. He gains that power when he does this to you. This is one of the reasons they want you to be single with no support system. There's nothing better than a woman who has to cancel her plans, stop working, cancel her girl's trip or turn down a position for advancement because she has a child.

    If you are a career driven woman and you have high aspirations as well as being very attractive, you should always be aware even if you are dating a male who appears to be on the same level as you. Males are easily triggered to view you as competition. Why? The nature of a male is wired to compete to pass his genes along. It is deep within their biological nature to compete. You being female does not assuage the trigger to compete. Males have a need to feel superior. So, always keep in the back of your mind that a male may use baby trapping to slow you down so he can reign above you.

I, not too long ago, dated a seven figure male. He owned a trucking company with 17 trucks in his fleet. He had been in business for 30 years. I dated him and worked for him. He was used to using his money and company to date younger women and have manipulative power over them. Very happy with his ability to seem like Mr. Big man, he would approach women flaunting his business as a way of being flirtatious. When he hired me and began to date me, he thought he could handle me in a similar way, flash a carrot in my face and I grovel at his feet.

What he had quickly come to realize, was my high level of intelligence in the trucking industry and his need for my assistance. It bothered him a great deal to feel like he needed a woman's help. Due to my 6 year long class A experience and my military background in logistics, I was very knowledgable about his industry. I could see where he was losing traction and control in his organization. This made him resent me and caused extreme jealously and competitiveness toward me. Even though he made significantly more money than I, had been in business for 30 years and lived longer than I, he was STILL intimidated by me and sought to sabotage his own workforce to cause me distress. He would start rumors, intentionally create conflict between other drivers and me, and hamper my work schedule. He would always tell me at random and odd times, "You might be smarter than me but you are not as sharp as me." I would always ask him why he continues to act as if he is in competition with me? He could never answer. He tried to hurt me with his jealousy by removing me from the schedule and playing with my paycheck. He felt I couldn't go anywhere in the industry because of my childcare needs. He felt he sniffed out a weakness that he could use to his advantage. Needless to say, that relationship has long ended. I took my power back and hurt his big ego when I walked away. I ghosted him for the second time and last time.

My advice: Do not have children unless you want them and can fully take care of them on your own or with your own support system. Do not allow male nature to poke out its ugly head to control and sabotage your life.

CHAPTER 30

THE HOSPICE CARE MAN

"Hospice means end-of-life care. The admission ticket is a diagnosis from a doctor that you have six months or less to live"

— Eleanor Clift —

An old man could come to you and say, "I am your father. I am sorry I didn't spend time with you and now I want to build a relationship with you." If this happens, there is a strong chance he is sick, screwed up plenty of relationships and now needs someone to assist him with his life. His life is on the decline and he will turn to children he abandoned or a new woman.

There was a nurse on TikTok who spoke about men going into the stroke ward in their early 40's. She spoke about how many of them were good looking and had good jobs. She further went to say that she often asked them "Where is your wife?"

She stated the reply was most often, "I've been a player and I never wanted to be locked down." She goes on to advise black men to wise up and marry a woman so she can "take care of him."

This is a revealing statement as well as scenario. The nurse promoted the message as if women need to dig into the worst places to find a male to take care of while basing her decision on his job and looks. This is not the 1930's. Women are not in need of basic necessities that only the LAW, at one point, prevented women from providing for themselves. The male, in this scenario, admitted never seeing the need for a wife to take care of him. In this statement, he reveals the only purpose a man has for a woman is for him to suck the life out of her and use her to fulfill a need he can not fulfill on his own. The male's expiration date would be a lot sooner if it weren't for women extending their lives with her help. Extending the male's life expectancy has caused great problems for males and the planet.

In 2009, ABC News made a report

detailing men's risk of stroke rising dramatically in mid-40s. This is interesting, because the nurse made her alarming TikTok video in the latter part of 2022. This affirms what ABC News reported. In the article, according to Dr. Michael Palm, assistant professor of neuroscience and experimental therapeutics and internal medicine at the Texas A&M Health Science Center College of Medicine, "The risk factors are most of the ones we start thinking about in older people—mostly cholesterol, but also smoking, high blood pressure and diabetes." It is also noted that the odds of stroke increase when men reach their mid 40's and "Silent Strokes' are most common in this group of men. Dr. Roger Bonomo, Director of stork care at Lenox Hill Hospital in New York City stated, "This is identifying a trend toward risk factors becoming more like older people in men in their 40's"

    Kevin Samuels, pseudo intellectual relationship guru, popularized the common sayings, "You'll Die alone, buy a cat" and "winter is coming." While the Manosphere, in general, popularized "you're going to hit the wall." This all speaks of a woman who was beautiful and gorgeous, able to float through life and then one day she gets old and no man is sexually attracted to her anymore. This is beyond interesting because if winter is coming and hitting the wall is happening for anyone, it would be the male. He knows this and desperately wants women to experience the life he lives of rejection and loneliness.

There was another woman on TikTok who warned women to look out for becoming a hospice care wife. These are males who know they are going to die already, and they seek out a woman to marry so they can leave all of the medical bills and debt to her while also having company and someone to take are of them in the meantime. There have been women left with large medical bills because of the males they married who were the true damaged goods.

My advice: Get rid of the fairytale idea of marriage. Financially protect yourself and do not fall for the banana in the tail pipe. Be sure to investigate how well he cares for himself because if you don't, you will inevitably become his care taker. If that is what you want for your life, by all means indulge. My suggestion to those of you who see yourselves as natural caretakers, please choose plants, animals, sea life and children to care for, not over grown adult males who add no value, have added no value, and will add no value to society.

CHAPTER 31

THE REVENGE MAN

"The paradox of vengefulness is that it makes men dependent upon those who have harmed them, believing that their release from pain will come only when their tormentors suffer"
— Laura Hillenbrand, Unbroken: A world War II Story of Survival, Resilience, and Redemption—

You must understand that men are born as uncultivated putty in need of a sculptor. Unfortunately, the sculptor is himself. One can not sculpt themselves if they have no self awareness, desire, vision or purpose. The average male needs someone superior to him to give him purpose. He is unaware his purpose on this earth is survival of the fittest and self mastery. He has to work for and earn every single thing he gets in this life. As I think of this, I don't believe it is he who is unaware of this but women who are unaware of this. Women think they are helping and being loving but they are ruining males when they try to save them from themselves and their reality.

Due to the nature of masculine energy, positive charge, which the male body is on the material plane, males can not exist in cohesion with other positively charged vessels. This is due to the nature of magnetism and polarity. Positive charges repel each other. This means males can not cohabitate and commune effectively. Effective cohabitation is organizing, planning and delegating tasks to efficiently run the home. Males don't do this. When they cohabitate they simply do male stuff and let it ride. Since positively charged ions and particles repel each other, it also explains the nature of males splitting themselves up into gangs. In a social study done on pre-teen children, the experimenter split up two groups. One group composed of 10 boys and another group composed of 10 girls. They were placed in a house without adult supervision. The boys immediately divided up into gangs. The girls did not. In addition to separating into gangs, males are also built to compete against other males. This reality isolates the male in his mind thus making him a lone wolf by nature. His lone wolf sentence does not make him an independent though. Forced isolation is not independence. This is nothing to feel sorry about. It's his raw nature and how it was always intended to be.

      This is not the biological reality of the woman though. She is communal by nature and she is the feminine vessel on the material plane. She is the negative/cathode end of a battery or magnet, multiple negatives or cathodes will NOT repel each other. This means women can cohabitate and commune effectively. They support each other and move together thus giving them eternal companionship and family. This makes the feminine independent of masculine energy and interdependent on feminine energy. Women are not lone wolves. The male on the other hand will either sink or swim. If he sinks, that is simply what was intended for him. This sounds cruel but it is the reality of his existence.

      It is this reality that has driven the male to subject, control and alter Mother Nature and all that is feminine. It is because the feminine does not allow him to exist at his lowest and most deficient state. Therefore, he has been driven to ensure his existence remains on planet earth. He has discovered many tactics and strategies to ensure that happens. Out of this need to exist is where the creation of artificial systems and philosophies rooted in male thinking arose. These anti-natural patriarchal systems then provided the male with rewards he did not earn. These rewards drastically altered his biological and psychological nature.

    These systems created a massive sense of entitlement in the male who began to believe the world owed him something. He was taught that all he had to do was go to work and provide and he could have the women of his choice. He was taught that women choose nice guys. On top of this, in exchange for his niceness and good job, he believed women would then owe him affection, catering, care, sex and so many other things. This sense of entitlement spawns a series of negative emotions that arise when he doesn't get what he believes is owed to him. Anger, rage, envy and hostility are just a few of these emotions. Because patriarchal religions conditioned males to believe they were created first and that Eve was made from a man's rib to cater to him, they began to believe women should accept them and meet their needs simply because they exist. Contrary to their delusion and entitlement, reality shows them that women are highly selective and have requirements. Women have eyes and don't just go for unattractive guys. Women have personalities and don't like boring companions. Many of these guys were not selected by their crushes because they lacked attractiveness and had nothing in addition to that. Therefore, when they get older and accomplished, they want to take their revenge out on women who didn't choose them when they had nothing. These guys will do many despicable things.

Here is a 7 year old reddit post made by a male admitting to getting revenge on a girl due to his weak and fragile ego. He also shows his inability to take responsibility for his own actions, behavior and self healing.

Here is a story of how I got my revenge on a girl I thought I loved. It is a long and emotionally exhausting tale.

"I was raised in a conservative household and therefore had unrealistic and fantastical ideals of love and relationships. I genuinely wanted my life to play out like a Disney fantasy. She was raised in a broken home, shafted from home to home and grew up with deep daddy and mommy emotional issues. I obviously only found this out too late - only after her issues had sucked me in and destroyed me along with her.

 Growing up I idolized her - our interests were similar and the fact I would only see her once or twice a month depending on which relative she was staying with - made her even more alluring to my young heart. While I was being raised up in a loving home, getting good results, graduating from high school to entering law school - she dropped out of high school and demonstrated typical behaviors of a damaged girl - sleeping around, dating much older men, no career ambitions, financial difficulties etc.

 Obviously, I know all of this now - at the time though, I thought she was just this sweet girl who was dealt an unfortunate hand - I told myself I didn't need to know the details - I would still 'save' her.

 By the age of 22 everything was going great in my life - I was on a good future path. However, one piece was missing…her.

I pursued her and eventually ended up in the back seat of a car having our first kiss together. While that was all great, my unrealistic idea of love implored me to seek a sign that she was in fact the 'one', that she was special. Believe it or not, the very next day I am in the city and I walk past her having a coffee with a friend. She sees me and calls me over and all three of us have a great time together. For me, this chance coincidence fucked up my life. I was now convinced she was the girl for me. I had to have her.

You can imagine the shock and despair that I felt then, when only a week later while on a late night phone call with her - she tells me she doesn't picture herself with me and that she doesn't want to pursue a relationship with me. From my point of view, I was perfect. What was wrong with me for her to reject me?! What had I done wrong?! What was missing from me as a person?! Did I not deserve her love?! What about this sign from above?! To my sheltered and naive existence, this rejection destroyed me to my core. I had never been rejected before, I was always happy and never suffered from depression or anxiety. This rejection changed it all. I suffered a breakdown. I cried for nights on end picturing our lives together and how it could never be. I analyzed everything about myself and critiqued every flaw searching for an answer as to why - when I was so sure this was right - this relationship failed.

Thankfully, I reached out to the right resources and followed the rules. I cut all contact with her. While this saved face with her, I was still hurting inside, privately. I told no one about this experience. I was extremely bitter and angry, not just at her anymore, but at life and love. I started to resent women and without realizing it started to passively aggressively react to them negatively.

It just so happens that about 3 months after cutting contact, I had a planned internship overseas. It was organized through my University and I would be staying at a local family's house. This was a fantastic situation to take my mind off of everything that happened and move on. It was to my disbelief (and now, looking back, unfortunate timing) that the family I was staying with had the most beautiful daughter I had ever seen in my life. One look at this woman made me forget about everything else wrong in my life. During my stay we got closer and closer and I learned that she had all the characteristics that I wanted in a partner. She was everything the other girl was not. Unfortunately, my bitterness and suspiciousness of women because of this past experience took a hold of me and I did something to this girl that destroyed any potential relationship I could hope for.

I blamed the original girl for this failed relationship. If I wasn't so emotionally damaged and crippled by my experience with her, I would have treated the overseas girl differently and maybe developed something - but no - even thousands of miles away - this girl was still ruining my life. It was now time to get my revenge.

Another year past with no contact - when through our social circle we finally met each other on a night out. By this time, I had improved myself considerably. I had addressed what I thought were my flaws to ensure she could never reject me again. That night we kissed again. She seemed so impressed with me now.

We slowly reconnected and started hanging out more. All the while, I was subtly getting her to fall in love with me. During the years of no contact, I had been in other short term relationships, I had slept with women and started to understand how to get them to click. It was exactly the opposite of what I was taught growing up. Respecting women, appreciating them, giving compliments - none of that worked. You had to be a man. You had to give off the impression that you were with three or four women on the side for them to respect you. I hated everything about this - but it worked. I eventually managed to get so close with this girl that she finally let me sleep with her. Immediately after she told me that no other man had ever made her cum that fast. This is the beginning of getting her attached to me emotionally and physically. She opened up to me and started to pour out her past. This is where I began to learn about her troubled past - it shocked me how little I knew of this girl. I had fallen in love with an idea of her - she was nothing like what I had pictured originally. The more I learned about her, the more I despised her past. The more I despised her as a worthless person. I felt ashamed I had let someone so weak affect me like she had. She was now in my hands to do with her as I will - and I wanted to make her feel the pain she had made me feel all those years ago.

    As months past, our relationship grew

stronger and stronger. I got her to open up to me sexually, making her do things she had refused to do with previous partners. She was now wanting to please me. She was now seeing everything she had missed all those years ago. She was proud of me.

This all culminated in a conversation where she wanted us to take the next step. During all of this - knowing I had no intention of having a real relationship with her, I had not told any of our friends or family about our relationship. She was now putting pressure on me - wanting to make it official to the world - wanting to tell her parents that we were now serious. Wanting to flaunt me to all her friends. Isn't it funny how things change? It was during this conversation that I told her I wanted nothing to do with her. I told her she shouldn't tell anybody about us because there wasn't an 'us'. I left her crying and cut all contact with her. That was over 9 months ago. We have not spoken a word or even seen each other in 9 months now.

I only bring this story up because we have a mutual friend's wedding coming up in the next week, and I am sure we will run into each other. I don't know how either of us will react or what will happen.

All I know is that I wish I never kissed her in the back of that car."

There is so much to gather from this confession. However, the most important thing to take away from this is idealizing other humans and living in a romanticized fantasy is self disappointment. He created this problem and punished her for what he did to himself. This is not the fault of the person whom you did not take the time out to learn and get to know. The male takes no responsibility for his own behaviors or thoughts and as a result, seeks to destroy you for being yourself and living your individual life.

Many guys will do this to women whom they have never dealt with but look like the types who did reject them. As you can see from this confession, males carry pain almost indefinitely due to their emotional weakness. Remember, studies show that males experience inflammation when they experience two or more breakups or living alone for an extended period of time.

My advice: Here you can see the male admits to studying female psychology and behavioral patterns. This is something women have not done with males. Women live in a land of total oblivion and delusion. You allow them to gain a one up on you due to your mental and emotional laziness. Stop idealizing relationships and men. Learn what Love is. The 5 Components of Love is a requirement for life as a woman. Learn who males are. The male is incapable of the 5 components of love and it will do you justice to not concern yourself with his ability to get it or not. The "Love, Men and Manipulation Decoded" workshop illustrates it all. Put yourself first and live in the here and now reality of life.

CHAPTER 32

THE REBOUND MAN

"Rebound "Relationships" are a great way to boost your ego while completely shattering an innocent person's life

— Anonymous—

We are all familiar with this guy. The guy who just recently broke up with a girlfriend or recently divorced and has an impacted self image. He is going through depression, physical pain and is newly single. The male has no direction or purpose without a woman in his proximity. Males are very oblivious to relationship problems due to their innate selfishness and lack of listening abilities. Typically, women go through the break up before she actually physically breaks up. As a result, the impact on her is very minimal. Even when the male breaks up with her out of nowhere, she still does not experience the physical pain the male experiences.

    The effect of this abrupt separation is the male finds himself in a desperate need to diminish his pain and occupy his mind with a distraction. This distraction is most often another woman. Sometimes you will know he's recently broken up and other times you won't. The rebound man is using your time, your energy and your availability to pacify himself. Most often, he is not serious about you. Sex is used as a stress reliever. So being able to relieve himself in another body is a great way to dim the pain.

Here is a reddit confession to support this claim.

I'm currently dating a girl and I know it's a rebound relationship, she doesn't think so. Does this make me a terrible person?

I[24M] recently got out of a 6 year relationship that I thought was going to last forever and now I'm just looking for some fun. I met this girl[19F] through a friend and she is fun and super hot and we have the best time together but she is a lot more invested in the relationship than I am. She isn't the person I want to spend the rest of my life with. I know that but I don't wanna tell her that because these four months have been wonderful. I even quit drinking after starting only two years ago. She's actually making me a better person but it's like she's molding me into a man that will in the future break up with her, meet another women, marry her and be a good and responsible husband and hopefully father. Am I deceiving her for not mentioning this or am I free of all guilt until she asks me the question "where do you see this relationship going?".

She is awesome, funny, excellent at board games, amazing in the sack and we actually bonded over our love of Pokemon but I don't see her as wife material or mother of my children material. I'm not saying she's not worthy or anything, believe me.. she is 10 levels above me in the 'who is a better human being' game but I don't see longevity here.

What are my obligations here guys?

Is this evil and if so, is this the level of evil I can get over with time?
She's very hot guys. :/
Do you see the deception, selfishness and utter confusion here? Males intentionally use you to fulfill their needs, they do not know what they want and they willingly lie to you and lead you astray. They know what they are doing to you. He did this to a 19 year old girl—took advantage of her naïveté. This is who they say their preferences are. Yet, you as a more experienced woman, will jump through hoops and drain yourself of your life force energy to get a male to validate you. You can be a 10, hot and 10 levels above him in the "who is a better human" category and he still will not validate you. The reason you have suffered in your life with males is because you have done little to no research, dismissed your own experiences and the experiences of other women and chocked it up to just "some men." Your faulty beliefs are the cause of your pain. Your desire to spare the male ego is the cause of your pain. Call a spade a spade. It's not "some men." It's the overwhelming majority of them. Some men are good men. They are of the minority.

      Remember the definition of delusion— a false belief or judgment about external reality, held despite <u>incontrovertible</u> evidence to the contrary, occurring especially in mental conditions. The majority of the world is mentally ill and they don't know it. Crazy people do not know they are crazy. Your delusions are causing your problems in life.

My advice: give him to time to reveal his true intentions with you. There are certain behavioral patterns you can see when a person is truly serious about you. This is detailed in The 5 Components of Love book and the Love, Men and Manipulation Decoded Workshop.

CHAPTER 33

THE POLY MAN

"I never tell one client that I cannot attend his sales convention because I have a previous engagement with another client: successful polygamy depends upon pretending to each spouse that she is the only pebble on your beach.
— David Oglivy—

The key word in this quote is PRETEND. Males have to play into the female fantasy which means they have to lie. Women demand these lies. Lies have an expiration date and can not be sustained for long periods of time.

The poly man is very easy to identify. He will typically be vocal and loudly push polygyny. If you are in the U.S. and pay close attention, you will notice, most often this male is of African American descent. Why? Because the Black American male is on the bottom of the socio economic totem pole. His moral deficits are due to his perpetual relegation to the bottom of Maslow's hierarchy in relation to males of other racial and ethnic backgrounds.

Although, the male is the male regardless of race or ethnicity, each ethnic group has a set of philosophies and politics which give their group of males a socioeconomic advantage. This advantage gives the illusion of male to male superiority and hierarchy. Unfortunately, for the black male, he has no governing philosophy that encourages him to improve his position on Maslow's Hierarchy of human needs.

He rejects philosophies of truth that white men have dominated because he believes in subjective truths. Instead of learning the philosophy of the winners, he studies the philosophies of the losers. He desperately tries to make the foundation of male nature the governing philosophy. He does this all while the dominating male has incorporated the foundations of female nature as the governing philosophy. By incorporating female nature into male governing philosophy, it automatically pushes those males to control and direct their nature. Males who make male nature their governing philosophy, effectively destroy themselves and everything around them much more quickly and evidently. Males innately know the woman is the power source. So, because of this, the poly male seeks to elevate himself on the backs of women instead of embodying the principles of women's nature within himself. Much like the pimp but this male has no leadership skill. Whereas the pimp is governed by a philosophy and uses discipline to catapult himself to the highest level of game in the underworld. The truly skilled pimp will typically leverage the resources of the woman to elevate himself above the underworld to play in the corporate league. He governs and controls his sex drive and is a business man.

The poly man needs to tap into the resources of multiple women to sustain himself without any desire to do business. He needs each woman to provide money, sex, housing, ego fulfillment and labor to make him comfortable. He wants threesomes and all. The poly man wants to showboat for the world to see him reap rewards for nothing and see that he is living the dream. He has no intentions to strive for anything besides living 100% off of women. He can not succeed in business, he does not want to work and he does not desire to provide anything for the women. He is totally defeated by his lack of will power, drive and the external competition in the free market.

My advice: Do not volunteer to help and reward a male who can not excel in the world of competition like he was designed to do.

CHAPTER 34

THE WHITE GIRL MAN

"White women are a status of success"
— *Nick Cannon—*

This male is specific to the Black American community. Black people in America are a different breed of people. To truly understand the differences of black people you must go back to the basics of understanding life and the living. Earlier in the book we spoke about the basics of biology. Living organisms have seven characteristics and one of the seven is response to a stimulus /the environment. Black people are human contrary to what slave times groomed the black human to believe. Slavery was a stimulus that altered the environment a great deal for them. Patriarchal philosophy is another stimulus add to that same altered environment. Black people responded to these stimuli by adapting biologically and psychologically to the prolonged introduction in the environment. This prolonged response has created an epigenetic change within the biological and psychological pathology of the black male. Due to black people enduring centuries of ego abuse along side the effects of patriarchal philosophy, black males have developed a deeper void and a stronger urge to protect their defeated fragile egos. This is because the black male is out performed in every area of life by his caucasian male competitors.

  Today, the black male has an utter disdain for himself because he is constantly reminded of his failures when he looks out into the world around him. Men are selfish by nature, so the way they view the world will almost invariably be through the lens in which they see themselves. When you take time to analyze this, what you will find is the utter disdain for self and the need to seek outwardly for what appears to have eternal value. They do this to make themselves look valuable when they are internally bankrupt.

  This is what leads and motivates the black male to seek white women, specifically.

White women have always been on a pedestal as a result of the white man's success at conquering the black male. Conquering and conquest is the nature of the male. No, it is not a sad case that the male is operating at his biological capacity. What is sad is that women have adopted male psychology and has become a weapon against herself, humanity and the planet for the sake male survival.

The black woman needs to accept that the black male's defeat by the white male is simply a loss. His loss truly only impacts himself. However, due to collectivist beliefs, she believes it impacts her. She believes it's her job to dedicate her life to saving her sons or another woman's son. But war, fighting, competing and destruction is what males do by nature and they do it by any means necessary. This is not the jurisdiction of a woman. She can not rescue him.

Patriarchy is a white man's game and in his game, the white woman is a token, a reward and a trophy to the black male. She is because it makes him feel as if he is closer to the white male in status. He feels this way because the white woman is in direct association with the white male and she was kept off limits at one point.

Laws against interracial marriage created an energy of desire. Desire is defined as a strong feeling of wanting or wishing to have something. Want can only come when one does not have. Slavery and disenfranchisement made the black male have strong feelings of wanting to be like white males and gaining access to his women. White males had power and the white woman was a symbol of that power due to her proximity to white men. Now, that the laws have been eroded and there's more free flowing energy between races and communities, black males feel as if they have accomplished something by dating white women. Even though they have not had to work to defeat white males in any way, this illusion is still something that strokes the black male ego.

Nick Cannon was recorded on his podcast with NOI spokesman, Rizza Islam, on how black males view white women.

Nick Cannon: " White women are viewed as success. Because in America we couldn't have you, my daddy couldn't have you and my granddaddy couldn't have you. I would get killed even looking at you. People—if they thought I whistled at you, they would murder me and they would beat me, drag me down in the street. So now, if I play for the NBA, I want them all. And I can afford them all. That's what they're thinking."

Rizza Islam: That's dealing with a slave master mentality

Nick: No, it's not. We are superseding it. I was a slave for this long so now I am going to take your woman. Your woman always wanted me. She always dreamt about me.

Rizza Islam: Well, She had you in the barn. She snuck and had you anyway.

Nick: I know, that's because it was forbidden. So now, that it doesn't have to be forbidden I am going to show I am the superior being.

This pathology is unique to the black male. The sad part about it is, he doesn't even realize the weakness in the statement, "now that it's not forbidden, I am going to show that I am the superior being." If he was truly superior, he would not have had to wait until the white male removed the forbidden law for him to show his superiority. His superiority would have been shown in spite of the law created by his caucasian competitors.

In his statement, you can clearly see the defeated self identity/ego and the need to be validated by what is perceived to have external value.

He is so evidently defeated. He is in desperate need to be seen as the winner in the delusional world he has created for himself. In this world of delusion, ONLY the white woman can stroke his ego and make him feel less defeated.

According to Pew Research, black men are twice as likely as black women to have a spouse of a different race or ethnicity (24% vs. 12%). This gender gap has been a longstanding one-in 1980, 8% of recently married black men and 3% of their female counterparts were married to someone of a different race or ethnicity.

Pew Research also states, "For blacks, intermarriage has increased most amongst those with no college experience. A recent study published by the National Council on Family Relations (NCFR) explored this aspect in interracial couples in the United States. Using data from the 2002 National Survey of Family Growth, the study analyzed almost 6,000 men and women between the ages of 15-44 who had never been married, over a period of ten years. The study found that:

- Marriages between a black husband and white wife were twice as likely to divorce as marriages involving a white husband and white wife. When adjusted for background aspects such as age at marriage and educational level, differences between black male/white female marriages and white male/white female marriages virtually disappeared in some cases. This suggests that, contrary to prior findings, the higher rate of interracial divorce between black male/white female marriages is not due to background factors.
  - Marriages involving a white husband and black wife were substantially less likely to end in divorce than marriage involving a white husband and white wife; the former pairing's divorce rate was 44 percent less than the latter.
  - Marriages including a black husband and white wife were more prone to divorce than those composed of black husbands and black wives. Black male/white female couples also had the

highest likelihood of divorce of all white/non-white marriages.
- While interracial marriage correlates to a higher rate of divorce, this parallel applies mainly to marriages involving a non-white male and white female.

Black male pathology is a very delusional and dysfunctional one. He will depend heavily on the woman to uphold his state of delusion in order for him to self sustain. It is impossible for humans to perpetually and indefinitely wear a mask to please others. This is a major cause for the lack of sustainability between the black male and white woman. His psychology is too dysfunctional.

My advice: Black Women, Do not be offended by their desire to date others. It speaks nothing of you and everything of him. If you are a white woman reading this, please understand he is pursuing you solely for ego reasons. He may treat you better or act differently with you. Please understand that it's not because you've done something special that a black woman didn't do or couldn't do action wise. The only thing you did do was bring him into closer proximity of the white male he's owned and defeated by. I advise you to take whatever he is willing to give you, money, cars, clothes, etc. Make him pay to get this ego need fulfilled. Men are incapable of love, it's transactional. We, as black women, are not upset with you for providing this service. We do ask that you stop competing with black women and adding insult to injury to boost your own egos. What does it do to your soul to know that you are denigrating someone else for a male? Competition is not the nature of women. We all have something to bring to the table for the advancement of nature, humanity and life. There is no need to shit on another woman for your own ego or a male's ego.

CHAPTER 35

THE LESBIAN MAN

"The sexual conquest is huge with men in terms of affirming themselves and their feelings of masculinity. That's a misguided kind of affirmation. That is not helpful, but that stuff happens."

— *Anonymous*—

Have you ever seen a chick who looks like a male, hair cut, sagging pants, tattoos and all? It's clear she's a stud. She hangs with the fellas and she behaves just like them but you look up one day to see her with child. How? Why? Hell, Who??? I have the answer to this question.

I have a Facebook associate whom I have met in person only once. He is an uber self proclaimed masculine, alpha man. He professes to be the expert on males and he once told me I don't know male psychology because I am not a man. He also doesn't believe in listening to women either. That is interesting because he made a post that read, "If a man gets a stud pregnant, that means he's attracted to men."

    I laughed because this is totally false. The male is a conqueror. He does not have sex for attraction only. It is a plus and an ego boost if he can have sex with whom he is attracted to but sex for males is a tool and the penis is a weapon. Men are instantly triggered to competition and they are triggered to pursue what they view as a challenge.

    The thing about the lesbian is she has taken her vagina off the market for male access. The male is now challenged to prove that he can gain access to her. He wants to show her that he possesses a special power to turn a lesbian woman "straight" by conquering her with his penis. In his mind, if you are so lesbian, why are you having sex with males? Why am I the one you had sex with? That says something about the power I have.

The stud is a lesbian, yes. However, the thing about the stud is she is extremely male identified. She looks like a male, walks, talks and acts like one. However, the male knows that no matter how much she portrays herself to be "male" she is still female. She still is territory to be conquered. So this triggers him to a conquering mentality. In his mind, he believes he is going to show her she can not be him.

She is not equal to him and he will prove that by making her a public spectacle. Impregnate her so the world can see her as confused and mentally weak because she was subdued and penetrated by a male. This is a major ego boost for him as it makes him feel he has psychological powers of finesse and strong penis power.

My advice: do not teeter totter on your convictions and do not give the male the satisfaction of victory by placing yourself in compromising positions. The male is not your friend, he doesn't see you as fine or better than another woman. He sees you as territory to mark. He will conquer and mark territory at any given opportunity. If you are in a relationship with a male and find out he "cheated" on you with a stud, do not question your worthiness as a woman. Do not question why he slept with someone you think is less attractive or less feminine. The fact of the matter is, the male is incapable of love and his conquests have nothing to do it. Stop beating yourself up over male behavior and stop fighting other women over it as well. You are worthy and only you validate you.

CHAPTER 36

THE PASSPORT BRO

"It isn't sexual tourism as wee know it now —they want to imagine they are having love affairs. (Ellen) is looking for a dream of being loved, caressed and looked after by someone who gives her no opposition,...The Damned"
— Charlotte Rampling—

In this new millennia, there is a phenomena of males being fed up with the dynamic of women not operating under the absolute desires and control of men. As a result, they have created communities online and movements to facilitate their imagined power of abandoning American women.

The original movement was MGTOW, Men Going Their Own Way. This was started by a group of white men who were fed up with white women and the "Feminist" movement. The male is extremely upset that the government has dismantled the artificial, anti natural controls called LAWS. These laws gave the male an artificial and manufactured advantage over women. Even though they have this advantage, they are also upset that there are laws that create artificial consequences for male biology that wouldn't be there if the laws were not created. One of these laws is Child Support.

The male is upset that he has to be responsible for his sexual behavior and reckless wild oats planting. He feels inhibited to operate in his natural form. These laws have to exist in this artificial environment because there would be too many offspring produced and abandoned. It's the male's biological nature to do just that. In a natural environment the male's opportunities to do this are dramatically reduced. There would be no need for such an artificial consequence if nature was allowed to rule because she places limits on the production of offspring to a great extent.

The laws that upheld such unnatural behavior to which the male had adapted, instantly disintegrated. This infuriated the male and caused him to disconnect and "go his own way."—MGTOW, Men Going Their Own Way. He proposed to stop dealing with women or deal with them on his own terms. As a spinoff, Red Pill, was created. This ideology is for men who didn't necessarily want to go their own way and stop dealing with women. These guys wanted to gain the advantage over women by attempting to educate themselves on female nature. Out of this grew the entire Manosphere where multiple sectors of males congregate to speak their frustrations, hatred and desires for control of women. Passport Bros is a newly created sector. These guys have tried going their own way but can't because they desperately need women. Although, this need prevails, they are trying to convince themselves they don't have this need. They learned some things from red pill and realized they do not have the funds in

America to play the hypergamy game. So, they opted to get their passports and go to third world countries, where the dollar has more value and the women are either impoverished or conditioned for male worship. They feel this will give them the women they need to feed their deficiencies. They run to these other countries because the cultures are still heavily patriarchal and women are still absent of the freedoms women possess in the U.S.

Just recently, shortly after I completed the initial draft of this book, Passport Bro Founder, Auston Holleman, posted frantically about being sought after by local Brazilians for his promotion of "sex tourism" in their country. He has been banned and run out of the country. They are taking their degenerate behavior and lack of desirability to other countries. The Asians have become aware of them and have labeled them LBH, which stands for Loser Back Home. OUCH! The Passport Bros have painted the women in other countries as "easy and cheap" to have sex with and use for their personal fulfillment. They deem them to be much easier than American women. The lack of respect for the country, culture and overall gifts to the world in terms of art, music and food is a slap in the face. They are there in these countries to find women who they believe are docile and receptive to their ill treatment. They do not want to develop themselves or improve on their deplorable characteristics. Instead, they believe they can arrive to these lands with uncultivated characters and use the value of the American dollar to exploit the resources of the foreign land, —human resources, their women. These guys want domestic servitude and are finding it increasingly more difficult to place women of their own land into these subservient positions due to their economic power and positions.

My advice: If you are a foreign woman, make sure you use him to get your financial needs met and get your US citizenship. If you are an American woman, his exodus is about him, not you. Don't be offended, be liberated.

CHAPTER 37

THE MIDLIFE CRISIS MAN

"Most people who experience midlife crises have spent their entire lives raising a family or working in a career. They haven't the time, or capacity, to ask the important questions in life. Eventually, something triggers the question. 'Is this all there is?"
— Mateo Sol—

Males differ a great deal from women. They have shorter life spans, more health risks, greater difficulty to achieve scholastically, lower listening abilities, along with an early loss of value or importance as they age. The reason for this is 1. There is a biological fragility in the Y chromosome, the SRY gene, that determines maleness. This fragility causes a wide range of different impediments that are unique to the male species. 2. because males are born without inherent value to society outside of passing genes along, the male has to find a way to add value to the planet, society and community on his own. This purpose has to come from within and he is empty on the inside. His life is heavily dependent on what he does and what he produces. This, indeed, presents a great challenge. Why?

Well, testosterone, the male sex hormone, is produced at very large quantities in the male compared to the female. As a result, his desire for sex is near uncontrollable. With a near uncontrollable urge for sex comes a near uncontrollable slew of thoughts. In this state, there is an absence of presence and attention. A male's attention is easily derailed when sex is introduced into the mix which provides a level of difficulty to be present in the moment.

I prove this, in real time on my YouTube show, The High Powered Podcast. Men, sometimes, call my show to address my talking points. I do not engage with their desire to argue. I simply derail their attention by introducing sexual suggestion into the conversation. This lowers intensity and aggression. It changes the conversation quickly. I remember watching Def Comedy Jam back in the 90's. There was a comic by the name of Andre Covington who said, "ladies, you want to know how to stop an argument? As soon as he gets to talking, you put a titty in his mouth! Treat him just like a baby…". Check it out here, https://www.facebook.com/watch/?v=5494211587264267. Begin at the 1:24 mark. I prove this works every time males call my show.

A man's life is heavily dependent on what he does, what he's able to produce, what value he can add to society, and his sexual desirability. Due to this, he recognizes his mortality much sooner than women. It weighs on him more because of the extreme fragility of the male ego. If the male has nothing else to be on the planet for, at least he has the ability to produce offspring. This bare minimum requires women to be open to him. This makes fertile female validation a top priority. To take his mind off of the mortality and/or depression, he seeks ways to cling to youth. He needs to cling onto things that have external value which can add to his perceived value. Even though external things have no real value and can add no real value to the soul or inner being of a person, these external things do add value to male egos.

They add value because the male does not live from the soul or inner place. He lives and expresses himself from the ego which is the external self. Money, cars, clothes, physique and youthful women are all external things a male seeks to cling on to give him a sense of vitality and life. He does not want to face the end and he does not want to feel worthless. The male is already born without a sense of value or purpose and his greatest fear is to die without having that. Increasing age with deteriorating health and vigor begins to erode that sense of purpose and value, thus eroding his life and presenting the image of mortality. This is one of the main reasons males tend to not want to retire. They want to continue working because once they stop working, they lose the spunk for life. Recent studies have shown that the male's social connections are tied to his occupation and once a male stops working, his social life leaves with the loss of employment. Then the process of isolation begins; another fear of the male.

All of these things motivate him to find a younger woman. This woman has to be young because she is full of life force energy, an energy of which he is depleted. Because the male is wired to seek validation from women, the woman acts as a mirror to who he is as a person. He needs a woman to mirror back to him youth, energy, and life since he is already fearing death. A woman of older age will only remind him of the end being near because she is also mirroring back to him. A young woman validates his youth. Even if the young woman is in it for money, his ability to bask in her youthful energy adds life-force to himself. This man is not in love or seeking love. He is seeking a feeling, a fantasy and energy which he can attach to for his survival of his mind, Body and ego.

My advice: Tax this man. Make sure your desires and financial needs are met. Males are transactional, be sure to tax for your services.

CHAPTER 38

THE SAVE FACE MAN

"The Noble art of losing face May some day save the human race and turn into eternal merit what weaker minds would call disgrace."
— *Piet Hein*—

Males are mostly alone and or around other males. Because they are not communal by nature and are, instead, competitors, they are always faced with a sense of peer pressure. They are always in a state of trying to one up another male or prove something to another male. Peer pressure can have just as strong effects on adult males as it has on teenagers. The pressure motivates a male to behave in ways he probably would not if he were not trying to save face for male validation.

Males will often ridicule other males for living, behaving or believing a certain way. Because of this, males often use women as tools to save face from the ridicule given by their peer group. Men, who are heavily driven by their egos such as the blatantly vocal Manosphere members, will seek out women who are more docile. They do this to broadcast to their peers how much control they have over women. He needs to show how much a woman bends to his will so that he can perform for and get validation from the bros.

Many times this type of guy can't handle the pressure of societal expectations. He will approach a woman and try to talk to her only to fulfill societal expectations of him. He is not really interested in having a woman. He simply will go through the motions but deep down wants to be alone or focus on the things he wants to focus on. When you are dealing with this type of guy, you will experience a lot of lack luster involvement. He will allow you to handle most things and run the household. He will let you make many decisions and just go along on the ride. He does this because he is not really happy in the set up but does not want to cause trouble, so he stays quiet. He is socially distant and busy with his own hobbies. He is just in it because he couldn't handle the pressure of rejecting societal expectations and living on his own terms.

Here is a 10 year old reddit post where a guy asks how to handle social pressure in getting girlfriend.

"I guess I have entered in that time of life when people expect me to be dating or have a strong relationship.
My mom is the main character in this. There is no fucking conversation that I have about school or anything social related that she wants to lead into me having a girlfriend.
It is not my priority to find one, it is not my main goal in life. I want to live free, to have things, to buy a house and a good car. I want to be happy and this is how I find happiness.

I am not very sure how to make you understand that.

Yes, I have had close relationships with girls in the past, but I felt it wasn't my thing to make it any more serious than being VERY close friends.

Yes, mom, some girls find me attractive, there are ones that have told me I am sexy. There have been other ones that have even told me straight up that they want sex. But, it is not my thing. I am not a womanizer and it is not me.

Why waste a girl's time when I will always know that I just want to be alone?"

My advice: Recognize the signs of a man who is just going along for the ride. Women can be so oblivious to men that she never recognizes when a male has checked out mentally or is unhappy with an arrangement. You have to be more aware of the world around you.

CHAPTER 39

THE ONLY FANS MAN

"It seems that women love to be exploited. When they are not exploited, they exploit the man."
— Malcom X, "The Autobiography of Malcom X" (1965)—

I think the name of this should instantly let you know who this man is. Porn has been something that has been part of this world for as long as there's been video. I'm sure it was here long before there was; it was just live.

This is a guy who is approaching you because he has the intent to manipulate you into doing Only Fans porn videos with him.

I will never forget when I was in my early twenties, I was actually a little chubby believe it or not. I did lose a lot of weight in the same time frame so I wasn't chubby for long. However, during the little chubby time, I was working at a convenience store not too far from where I lived at the time. I worked the 2pm-10pm shift and I was at the beginning of my day on this particular day. A guy walks in to purchase some things, I total it up, bag it and processed his payment. When it was all said and done, he handed me his card and said, "You are beautiful. I am a movie producer. I think you'd be a great model for the industry." I then asked him "what type of movies do you produce?" He replied, "adult films." Ha! No sir. At this time there was no Only Fans or Porn Hub, but it was still DVD era. Same thing. I felt in my spirit he was on some bullshit. Clearly, I was right.

About a year and a half ago, there was a popular controversial YouTube influencer who made a name for himself by criticizing ethnic women. His fame came from verbally tearing them to shreds. Over the years his fall from grace has been quite dramatic. Prior to his fall, I had been invited on his show to discuss several topics. Everything was fine until it wasn't. One day we got into a major disagreement and had a public fall out. Needless to say, there was no communication for a few years.

One day in 2019 or 2020, I made a Fb video expressing that if a male wanted to be involved with me sexually, the minimum fee would be $3000 to even think about it.

On social media, you have the ability to control what audience sees your videos and posts. Being who I am, of course, this was a public video. Well, not too many days after I posted it, I got a random call from this YouTuber. I had not seen or heard from him in 3 years since the fall out. He was expressing interest in collaboration and letting bygones be bygones. Well, that's interesting, especially given the timing.

After further listening over the course of a week, it had become evident that he had now gotten involved with Only Fans making extremely degrading content. He was attempting to solicit me to do it with him by offering to pay the $3000 fee I spoke of on my fb video. So, essentially, what happened was someone saw my video and reached out to him to inform him I was selling pussy. He thought it was an opportunity to sleep with me as he already had expressed an interest years ago with no success. In his mind, this was his opportunity to do so. As you see there was no coincidence in him randomly reaching out not too long after that Facebook video. Needless to say, I did not oblige as there is no and was no amount of money I was going to accept to sleep with him. The intent to sleep with me had more to do with image and character assassination than it had to do with any form of sexual attraction.

Many of these guys will sit back in the bushes and wait for the perfect time to strike the iron. Many guys have patience, most others do not. It is very easy to deal with guys who have no patience. because their intents and purposes are easily spotted and caught early. The red flags they leave are very blatant. The patient guy is like Aleix Segura Vendrell, world record holder, for holding his breath under water for 24 minutes. That is synonymous to a lifetime in terms of the brain going without oxygen. A skilled guy, who may have a Machiavellian Dark Psychology personality type, will wait patiently for YEARS to set you up and strike. However, the reward has to be worth the investment. Only fans is not worth the investment of years of waiting. It is too easy to play the numbers game and find a woman who is interested in doing so. If a male is already married, he may have to place a little more investment of time, money and energy to persuade his wife to do it but for the most part, many women out there don't need much convincing; they are already interested in doing it.

You look good enough to be used as a spectacle.

My advice: don't be offended, just figure out his intentions up front.

CHAPTER 40

THE BUILD-A-BEAR MAN

"Men have to figure life out."
— Jordan Peterson—

The unfortunate reality is women have been sold wolf tickets and lied to about males and love. Women give all they have in the value of themselves through self sacrifice in the name of love. Women believe love hurts and love works against their own best interests. This is toxic believing. Love does not hurt. However, her idea of love causes her to prove her worth and value in exchange for love from a male. In the process of doing so, she is mentally, emotionally, spiritually and, often times, financially destroyed. She believes this is all in the name of love. If you have read my book, "The 5 Components of Love" and have gone to my workshop, "Love, Men and Manipulation Decoded" you will know, unequivocally, that males are not capable of love. So, to seek to acquire something from the male that he does not have and or have the ability to manufacture is a losing battle. The male knows he is not capable of love and it's his best kept secret. He allows you to believe he can and uses his inability to love as a scarce commodity that a woman must earn if she is the 'RIGHT' woman for him. The male sees this as a complete advantage. Because he is incapable of love and penis is used as a weapon to conquer, love is the perfect subterfuge.

The life of a male is very difficult because of his natural born impediments. What do I mean? Male children face greater challenges in surviving in the womb than female offspring. They face a greater risk of in-utero death. They are 14% more likely to die of premature birth than girls. It is also noted that girls develop faster in the womb than boys. As a result, they have greater risk of complications than girls at the same gestational age. According to research performed by Adolescent Psychiatrist, Sebastian Kramer, "The male fetus is at greater risk of death or damage from almost all the obstetric catastrophes." He goes on to list the issues male face before birth. Perinatal brain damage, cerebral palsy, congenital deformities of genitalia and limbs, premature birth and still birth are much more common in boys than girls.

   He states the impediments males face are "wired in" and persists from birth to the grave. This is why a male's self image/ego is so weak and so fragile. The woman is strong. The stronger and more desirable the woman, the more it highlights his own fragility. A male gets his biological validation from his access to women. The male gains access to power through the woman. Kramer also mentions that "males are attempting something extra all throughout life." Without the woman the male is carrying very burdensome load. Unfortunately, Patriarchy added these additional burdens on to the male which requires him to take on the responsibility women were naturally meant to carry.

As the extreme difficulties of life continue to be placed on the male, many of them will fail at life because the lack enormous amounts of help from other males or women. Patriarchy only created a wheel chair society for males that support resource, ego and sexual attainment and domination. It ignores, mental, emotional and spiritual support. Thus, leaving males to be heavily dependent on themselves or women. That's a problem because women can't and won't be the help they need because

1. She is overburdened with a multitude of responsibilities because of the unnatural nuclear family structure that eroded her network of support. Now, all of the critical labor is on her which depletes her energy reserves. She doesn't have the emotional reserves for herself and breaking down mentally herself.

2. She has been conditioned to believe the male is the stronger sex, head of the household and leader. This means, as a leader, he is responsible for providing all of

the emotional, financial and spiritual things biologically given to women. She is unaware this is her duty because of societal conditioning. She is conditioned to see the male as superior and more capable than herself.

3. Other males will not provide him help because they are struggling with the exact same things he is struggling with and they do not have the intuitive skills or abilities to help him. So the male has been given a freedom he can not handle. Freedom means the ability to self govern and the male is not designed to be or do either, respectively.

Males created patriarchal societies to force women by aggression and psychological conditioning to lower her access point so the male can survive off of her energy. However, he was only surviving physically and financially while he was being obliterated emotionally. The woman is not aware she is being used in this way because she has been sold on love, romance and a knight in shining armor. These were productions funded and controlled by males.

Women have long complained about helping a male with his education, business, children, hygiene, health etc. to build him into the man who will love her. Only to do so and see him leave her for another woman. She has never understood why. It is because she was an easy stepping stool to assist him in reaching a level he was not capable of reaching on his own.

He did it to build himself to a point he is able to approach the type of woman who will mask his deficiencies and add external value to his social standing. All in pursuit to inflate his ego and sense of importance. Males do not value what they do not work for. They are internally and eternally aware of their own deficiencies and anything that is given to them freely and without effort, in essence, destroys their self image more because it makes them feel handicapped. They feel like charity cases, socially, financially and educationally retarded.

God, the all knowing and almighty, higher power being, is supposedly male, He. Males are supposedly made in "his" image. Women were said to come second and be beneath the male. Because of these philosophical beliefs, it makes him even more angry to accept help and still be seen as superior when the "weaker sex," a woman, helps him do what he was told she is not capable of doing.

As a woman, if you select to take on the project of building a bear of a male, you will be taking on a risk that is far greater than any reward than you can receive.

Galileo, Italian scientist, stated, "you can not teach a man anything, you can only help him find it within himself."

Women are too busy believing they are helping men by giving them energy, time, and resources. You aren't. You are only creating resentment in him because he innately understands and knows the existence of his own deficiencies, impediments and limitations. You make him feel even more worthless by giving to him, hence why he leaves you for the woman who kept herself out of his reach.

My advice: do not build males even if they cry, beg and plead. Allow him to sink or swim on his own effort or lack thereof.

CHAPTER 41

THE "PICK ME" GIRL MAN

"I hate women like that. They are so desperate for the attention of men, that they'd willingly betray and harm members of their own sex."
— Sarah J. Maas—

Patriarchal societies have flipped nature on its head and turned the tables around 180 degrees. By nature, women choose males. The male does not have the power to choose a woman to pass his genes along. The woman is the natural governor and selector of males. However, under the laws and structure of patriarchy, the artificial resources, fiat currency, was given to the male to hoard. This forced women into a subservient position to await the male to give her access to the resources he was now in control of. This gave him an unnatural power to choose. Provision of resources was then connected to a man's "love" which he now had the power to choose to whom he would give it.

By nature, women were in control of nature's resources. She was given dominion over the planet to maintain its life and keep it regenerating to sustain all life on the planet. When women held the resources, she held the power to reject males and reduce her exposure to males. This posed a problem for males because they depend on and need females for their very survival. Therefore, stripping women of their right to independent resource control, forced women into a state of "hypergamy" which is a response to the anti-natural stimulus of patriarchy's economic philosophies. These philosophies are rooted in competition, hoarding, ownership and control which are all the foundations of male psychology and male nature.

Due to continued exposure to these anti-natural philosophical principles, women's biology and psychology were epigenetically altered to adapt to this new environment. Women have been exposed to male philosophies for so long that she has a male psychology in a female body. She does not know how to be a woman. Her idea of womanhood is predicated on what she believes a male wants in return for the artificial resources he possess and "love." Hence, the creation of the "Pick Me." The pick me is a woman who is fully functioning in the male psychology of being chosen. Therefore, her position is 100% self sacrifice to her own detriment and the detriment of other women and girls. She does this to be selected and validated by males. Earlier in the book, I mentioned how males are naturally validated by women as they depend on her selection of him to affirm his existence by providing him an opportunity to pass his genes along. One of the artificial tactics used by males to force women to seek validation from them is the creation of the Surname, Miss, Ms. and Mrs. Women who do not have a Mrs. in front of their names are harshly judged by society and seen as defective. This is a systematic creation and does not exist in the nature of women. In untouched nature, the male is the one who lives this harsh existence. If a male has not been able to attach himself to a woman, it is an indicator that he is defective as his ultimate goal in nature is to use the woman's body as a vessel to keep his genetic line flourishing.

If he can not do this because he has not been chosen by a female, it is a strong indicator of lack of genetic desirability. Women do not live this existence. So, males created the concept of marriage to ensure the male does not have to live this horrid existence and AT LEAST have a wife. However, they packaged, marketed and sold this image as a benefit and necessity of the woman so she would be psychologically bullied into not rejecting males. The most effective strategy used to ensure this worked was to attach these principles to religion and make god a man. If women see god as male and not a woman, she would willingly self sacrifice for male survival through the belief that she is pleasing and obeying God. Out of this conditioning grew the behavior of women jumping through hoops and hurdles to be picked by males. This is all because it is seen as what a good woman does. People, in general, are afraid of not being seen as a good person.

The male now has the woman where he wants her. The male is not interested in the pick me because she poses no challenge to his biological nature of earning reward. However, competition, conquering and dividing are all part of the biological nature of the male. So, he does seek to use the pick me to push and advance his own self interest by using her as a weapon to conquer and destroy women he does not have access to. Through the tactics of guilt tripping, shaming, colorism, racism, and more, he is able to accomplish this. The women who have been poisoned by these ideals relish in the validation and positive reinforcement that strokes her ego. Remember, males have a brain wiring that works on a reward system. Males must be trained like dogs and they are aware of this. However, the pick me has effectively become the dog for the male. In the great words of Tupac, "You wonder why they call you, bitch." If a man is in total agreement with a woman, pushes her points of view and applauds her overall, this is a sign of her being used as a tool and weapon. If he is seeking you and agreeing with your every point, you are a pick me. Males will never agree in unison to the facts of their existence because it does not validate their sense of worthiness on the planet.

My advice: do not sacrifice yourself or other women to uphold the delusions of the male world because this is destructive to all life on planet earth. Learn to love yourself and add value to the world.

CHAPTER 42

THE CHESS PIECE MAN

"You can only win the game when you understand that it is a game. Let a man play chess, and tell him that every pawn is his friend. Let him think both bishops holy. Let him remember happy days in the shadows of his castles. Let him love his queen. Watch him lose them all."
— *Mark Lawrence*—

It is well known that males simply do not have the power that women posses. Women possess sexual power and males are easily captivated by it. As a result, a woman can bring down the defenses of a male with not very much effort. Males know other males and understand the nature, intent and ruthlessness of each other. Therefore, they are typically on guard in regard to other males.

Men who are driven to take over businesses, gather intel or get into places easily and unnoticed will typically need the power of a woman to do so. Great civilizations crumbled at the hands of a male's weakness to sex.

Men need women to make their music videos, commercials, and organizations look more appealing and alluring. So the number one intention of this male when he's approaching you is to have you be a piece in a scheme he is trying to put together. Only a beautiful, seductive woman can get into high roller places. Many nations have fallen by the use of a woman as a chess piece to sabotage an operation or gather intel.

I encourage you to pull up the lyrics to Lil'Wayne's "Mona Lisa" to see how well he details a robbery with the use of women.

My advice: Think about the lives of others you will be impacting if you participate in the games of destroying other lives.

CHAPTER 43

DARK PSYCHOLOGY PERSONALITY TYPES

"It is the individual who is not interested in his fellow men who has the greatest difficulties in life and provides the greatest injury in others. It is from among such individuals that all human failures spring."
           —Alfred Adler—

This book has been about the motivations and intentions of the male to pursue, subdue and use you. Here, are the personality types and characteristics of a person that you can connect to the intentions of them.

There is what is called a Dark Psychology Triad. A triad of the three negative types of personalities that will impact a person negatively. The triad consists of psychopathy, narcissism, and Machiavellians.

PSYCHOPATH

Let's begin with Psychopathy. Psychopathy is a neuropsychiatric disorder marked by, poor behavioral controls, deficient emotional responses,, commonly resulting in persistent anti-social deviance and criminal behaviors.

If we were to break each aspect of this definition down to scientific evidence of male behavior and nature, you will probably be shocked at what you're being faced to see.

First, let's understand the brain is the central processing unit for human beings. A human's behavior is controlled by the information the brain receives from internal and external environments. Each area of the brain is critical to what humans are and are not capable of. The volume/disk space of the brain will be indicative of what functions the human cpu is able to perform.

In regard to the definition of psychopathy, let us begin with poor behavioral controls. Control and behavior are the key words here. Humans are creatures of emotion not logic. That is not necessarily a bad thing, however, many people lack a thorough understanding of what emotions are and their purposes. Patriarchal philosophies have demonized emotions and painted them as a form of weakness. In actuality, emotions are a form of weakness for the male because of his inability to control them. This is not true for women. Women's brains are wired to control emotion. All humans are emotional. Emotion is nothing more than a chemical released in the body which are a result humans to responding to external stimuli. Chemicals are energy. The release or inhibition of chemicals in the body result in a wide range of emotions. These emotions range from depression, anger, anxiety to happiness. These states of being are chemically driven and controlled by the human cpu. The human is composed of chemicals. Therefore, the control of these chemicals and states of being resulting from the release or inhibition of them is what is being examined in the first part of this definition.

The most important regions of the human CPU for this discussion The Orbital Frontal Cortex and the Amygdala. The orbital frontal cortex is associated with emotional control. The Amygdala is where emotions are processed. Studies have shown that women have significantly larger Orbital Frontal Cortices Volume in relation to the amygdala than males. This is important to know as this cortex is involved with the ability to control, govern or inhibit one's emotions. This information alone shatters the patriarchal assertion that women are more emotional than men and males are more logical. This has been a lie from the beginning. A lie designed to oppress and limit the woman.

So, let's think about this for a moment. Without a clinical psychiatric concern, the male, by normal nature, is already predisposed to psychopathic ways due to a reduced ability to control his emotions and behavior. This should make you aware of your safety when you are surrounded by a sex whom you know does not have the disk space or functionality to control his behavior.

Now, let's add in the effect testosterone has on the brain. Studies have revealed those who were given a dose of testosterone made quick impulsive decisions. This is because testosterone inhibits the functionality of the prefrontal cortex, where cognitive control, attention and impulse inhibition are regulated. In other words, testosterone overrides judgment and effective decision making. Males have 15 times more testosterone circulating in the blood stream than women of similar age.

Let's process this. In a normal male, his ability to control his behavior and emotions are reduced and testosterone causes him to be an impulsive decision maker.

What other effect does testosterone have on the brain?

According to more studies, testosterone plays a significant role in the arousal of the following behaviors, anger, verbal aggressiveness, competition, dominance behavior and or physical violence.

Now, let's consider this factor, the male has a reduced ability to control his behavior, testosterone incites impulsive behaviors and testosterone arouses anger, competition, dominance behavior and physical violence. This is all normal behavior without a clinical concern for psychopathic tendencies.

Patriarchal philosophies and religions conditioned the world to prefer male children over female children. It conditioned you to believe women needed to be controlled and males needed to be free and out front. It conditioned you to believe boys were easier to raise than girls which resulted in you being less attentive. Due to these false beliefs, women inflated the world with more males than females resulting in a chaotic crises of a gender imbalance. This imbalance created 70 million more males than females in the eastern regions.

Women naturally have more self governing control than males. Therefore, the natural governor was, is, and will always be the female species. So, what will happen if the governing bodies dismantle all of these artificial controls that are preventing males from terrorizing the globe? How will women control a population of aggressive males who outnumber them by 70 million? They are horny, high levels of testosterone and large numbers of males competing for a small amount of women and food. If you read the history of the wars that took place in Somalia, you will understand why there is a rape issue that prevails. Males were weaponized to attack women during the social and economic downturn. The males were given khat to heighten their testosterone and sex drive. They used this to regularly rape women to tear down their opposition. What do you do when there is nothing forcing the male to control his behavior when his brain won't? Studies affirm that the Anterior Insula Cortex is the region for empathy. Studies also suggest testosterone has an impact at lowering empathy in males. So far, we have only discussed what is normal behavior for the male.

These behaviors exist with normal volume of the amygdala. This type of brain wiring explains why 93% of all imprisoned persons are male.

So, with this sort of predisposed marker for destructive behavior, it should frighten you that an actual psychopath has a reduced volume of the Amygdala in terms of his brain function. The reduction of this region reduces his emotional responses.

Psychopaths are pathological liars, poor judgment and failure to learn from experiences, impulsivity, lack of remorse or shame, grandiose sense of self worth, manipulative behavior.

According to Dr. Wilem H.J. Martins, MD, PhD, "Psychopaths have a deep wish to be loved and cared for. This desire remains frequently unfulfilled, however, because it is obviously not easy for another person to get close to someone with such repellent personality characteristics. Psychopaths are at least periodically away of the effects of their behavior on others and can be genuinely saddened by their inability to control it. The lives of most psychopaths are devoid of a stable social network or warm, close bonds." -Psychiatric Times.

Based on this excerpt and the science related to the normal human male brain, a psychopath and "normal" male are not polar opposites. This is even more alarming when you factor in the reality there is a rise in single lonely men and an over abundance of males on the planet. Patriarchy has created a grandiose sense of self worth in the average male by way of crowning him as head of household, the first human created and man being made in the image of God. All while diminishing the value of the woman. This is now further exacerbated with the near mainstream concept of the Manosphere, a place where males can express their frustrations and assert their superiority and dominance over women.

Based on this information, I ascertain that is plausible to assume that anti-natural philosophical stimuli creates a dysfunctional human being that exhibits disorders like psychopathy. Based on the science, there appears to be more psychopaths in the world than 'experts' are willing to admit. A clean criminal record doesn't mean someone has never committed a crime. It simply means they were either 1. Never caught 2. Given grace or 3. Have connections in higher places that can cover up or clean up the evidence. The same goes for a clinical diagnosis of psychopathy. If we know males do not go to doctors or seek therapy, the lack of a clinical diagnosis for psychopathy or a crime associated with it does not indicate the absence. Psychopaths have a LOT of the same traits as a normal functioning male. Psychopaths are just more severe.

NARCISSISM

Next, we have a Narcissist. Narcissism is also a personality DIS ORDER. A Dis order can only exist, with the exception of DNA copying errors, when an organism is exposed to unnatural stimuli for extended periods of time. Thus, epigenetically adapting and mutating into a new form of itself. In the set up of this global world, there are a myriad of anti-natural stimuli created that have impacted the world and human behavior globally. We've spoken about the intentions of this male in chapter 17, but now we will focus on his psychological make up.

The term narcissist was created based on a Roman story of Narcissus and Echo. Narcissus had a habit of rejecting potential lovers and after rejecting, Echo, Narcissus had been punished to fall in love with something that could not love him back. He fell in love with his own reflection in a pool of water. Although, this is a mythological story, mythology often found its origins in the experience of man. Therefore, stories like Narcissus and Echo, reflect the behavior of man which inspired the writing.

Over the years, the traits of Narcissus began to be recognized as a personality type with actual characteristics. The description of this personality type first was described as a 'God Complex' by Welsh Neurologist, Ernest Jones, close friend of Psychosexual Psychologist, Sigmund Freud. He described the traits in his paper, "Essay of Applied Psycho Analysis," as aloof, self-admiring, over confident, inaccessible, auto-erotic, self-important, exhibitionistic, and a high need for uniqueness. The patriarchal idea that man was created in the likeness and image of god, as well as being the original human could definitely be said to be the cause of these self centered beliefs in males. As males are the primary sufferers of NPD. If you listen to the Pro Black Sector of Males, you will constantly hear, "we are god." Psalms 82:6-7 is a common scripture they like to use to affirm their God Complex beliefs. "I have said Ye are gods. All of you are children of the most high But Ye shall die like men."

Cultures all around the globe, emphasize the importance of males while diminishing the value of women and girls. These cultures cultivate women and girls to cater to and serve males as if they are god. So, it is to no surprise why males act, behave and believe in this God Complex manner; this prolonged anti-natural stimulus has been injected into the world environment for centuries.

Mayo Clinic describes those who are affected by NPD to "have an unreasonably high sense of self importance, seek too much attention and want people to admire them. People with this disorder may lack the ability to understand or care about the feelings of others. But behind this man of extreme confidence, they are not sure of their self-worth and are easily upset by the slightest criticism."

Let us process this statement while considering what we have already learned about biological and psychological nature.

Statistically, it is said that only 7.7% of the population is affected by NPD and of that 7.7%, 75% of them are male. I find this very difficult to believe in terms of such the low estimation of the general population percentage. Why? Before we get into that, let's present the detailed list of traits of a narcissist.

-exploitation of others for self need fulfillment

-A heavy focus on success, power, and of being   the perfect mate.

- an inability or unwillingness to recognize the needs and feelings of others
- Envious of others and suspicion of the envy from others.
- Entitlement to special treatment and privilege

- Inflated achievements
- Arrogant and braggadocios
- Unreasonably high sense of self worth and importance.

Narcissists have extremely inflated yet fragile egos. The ego, is one's self identity. It is the FALSE/EXTERNAL self. A person's ego self is associated with all things external such as favorite foods, hobbies, clothing, colors, sexual access and desirability, jobs, salary, physical appearance, accomplishments, sports teams, etc. People with large egos heavily depend on these external things to support them and speak for them. When these large egos are fragile, criticism of these external things can break the confidence of the ego driven person.

Here are some ways a person with NPD will respond to criticism.

-become impatient or angry when they do not receive what they believe they are entitled to.

-have difficulty managing their emotions and behaviors.

-difficulty handling stress and adapting to change.

-react with rage and contempt. Belittle others to make themselves appear superior

-have secret feelings of insecurity, shame, humiliation and fear of failure.

Now, going back to WHY I have a hard time believing only 7.7% of the general population is effected by NPD. 24% of the world or 1.8 billion people identify as Islamic and 31.1% identify as Christian, 2.3 billion identify as christian and .2% of the population, 15 million is Judaism. These are patriarchally dominated religious philosophies that effect 55% of the globe.

These religions center the male as of the utmost importance. These religions are the center of this artificial world which goes against the world where nature is the center of its existence. How is it possible for 55% of the globe to be dominated by male centered religious philosophy and only 7.7% of the general population be affected by over inflated self identity?

Going back to Sebastian Kramer's research in regard to the male disadvantage that is wired in from infancy and persists to the grave. The male has a myriad of impediments he has to surmount throughout life and has little to no importance on the planet. Because of this innate inferiority, the male's most driving need and urge is to feel a sense of importance. This is of far greater intensity in the male than the female because the female is born biologically needed. She nurtures and takes care of offspring, she is needed to maintain society and nurture life. The woman is innately necessary as her continued participation in life sustains life on the planet.

The male simply does not have comparable importance. So, think. 100% of males, have the same biological foundation, only important for passing their genes along. Because of this biological reality, males have a glass ceiling which biologically makes obtaining sexual access the final reward. Therefore, by default, the male's sense of importance or validation for his existence is predicated on whether or not a woman chooses to participate in sex with him. The male's value is heavily dependent on his biological nature.

So, one of the traits of narcissism stated above is -entitlement to special treatment and privilege.

Patriarchal religions and societies have created an artificial world which will allow the male to get his needs met at the expense and sacrifice of the woman in order to sustain his life and existence. Laws and religious doctrines have made women give rewards to the male and allow him to exist without controls.

This, as result, created an unnatural psychological and behavioral response in males, similar to the response of the mice in John Calhoun's, Universe 25 experiment. In this experiment, John Calhoun, wanted to see what effect would having all of your needs met and catered to have on life. The Result? The mice recklessly reproduced, became violent, broke off into gangs and ultimately collapsed the artificial environment called, Universe 25. The mice essentially forgot how to be mice in this environment.

This is the same altered behavioral patterns of the human male as a result of this artificial environment run by patriarchal philosophies.

Therefore, with the biological nature of a male being wired to be ultimately concerned about his importance, an artificial world was created to give him this sense of importance with little to NO EFFORT. Having a religious belief that paints god in the image of himself, it makes it hard to believe only 7.7% of the population is effected by NPD. However, it does make sense that 75% of this "7.7%" are male and not female.

The next trait is a
-heavy focus on success and power. -

Going back to the biological science on the male in reference to testosterone. Testosterone is confirmed to drive competition in males as well as increase when he is the winner of the competition. Power, in context of testosterone is defined as physical strength and force exerted by something or someone. Testosterone, not only, gives males their strength but also their identity to manhood. Testosterone is a steroid which ultimately differentiates him from female. Therefore, a heavy premium is placed on making testosterone and the behavioral patterns associated with it the center of manhood.

Because testosterone induces competition and is higher amongst the winners of said competition, males, by nature, place a heavy focus on success and power. This success and power is in direct relation to testosterone levels which define male existence. Success and Power exist on the bottom echelon of Maslow's Hierarchy. This drives the territorial nature of males and their need to hoard resources because males operate with a scarcity mentality.

So, now add in the fact that patriarchal societies have in place philosophies which are rooted in hoarding nature's resources. They created and hoarded artificial resources and made the majority of work environments male dominated including politics. You should now be able to see how the male became entitled. His sense of entitlement is an adaptation to this artificial environment. This is how the majority of the world is functioning. After taking all of this into consideration, it makes it hard to believe only 7.7% of the world is effected by NPD.

The next trait is an

-inability or unwillingness to recognize the needs and feelings of others.

Multiple studies have shown that normal males have lowered empathy. In addition to lower empathy, according to a team of researchers at Cambridge University, multiple studies conclude that women are far better listeners than males. In women, parts of the brain linked to emotions, calculating risks and the ability to listen were more prominent. More research performed on undergraduate medical students showed that females scored significantly higher for non-verbal communication. The male students frequently interrupted the patients after the beginning of the interview.

This is very profound as listening is the gateway to understanding. Males have less ability and desire to actively listen. Without the ability to listen to understand there can be no recognition for the needs and feelings of others.

In addition to this, the biological nature of the male is to seek to get his needs fulfilled at at the expense of others, as he operates within the law of self preservation in the lower echelon of Maslow's Hierarchy of Human needs. He is perpetually there due to his biological impediments and dependency on others to sacrifice themselves for his survival. This makes him less caring about the needs of others. Therefore, by nature, the male's personality is already bordering NPD.

In the wake of Red Pill, Black Pill, MGTOW, passport bros and the entire Manosphere, there is rhetoric being pushed that the woman's purpose on the planet is to serve man and she is out of place. This triggers them to put her in her place. In their mind, feminism, is the cause of society's destruction. In other words, giving human rights to women is the cause of the destruction of the world.

'Women have been brainwashed to achieve great things. She has been hoodwinked into financially providing for herself. She has now made it to a place where she thinks she doesn't need a man.' -Anonymous Manosphere Nutcase-

These are the talking points of the Manosphere. Passport bros are going over seas to exploit women who they believe are vulnerable for sex.

The sex trafficking industry is a $150 billion industry. The patrons of this industry are male. If males were not biologically wired to exploit others for their own gain, sex trafficking would end. It would be too many empathetic males who would put their desires for sex aside and rescue underage girls who are there, clearly, against their wills.

These are just more in-depth explanations of the traits between narcissism and nature.

What about the response to criticism of the natural male vs. the clinically diagnosed NPD male?

A common response to criticism as a trait of narcissism is difficulty managing their emotions and behaviors. Well, we have already gone into the science of testosterone overriding the orbital frontal cortex. It cancels the function for the normal male to control his behavior thus increasing his impulsive behavior. So, once again, by nature, the male exhibits traits of NPD. 55% of the globe is indoctrinated with patriarchal beliefs of god being man, male's being superior and the aggressive nature of males as being a trait of manhood.

Another NPD response trait is

-becoming angry or impatient when they don't receive what they believe they are entitled to.

We've already seen how the male's sense of entitlement was created. We also see testosterone's effect on his amygdala. It induces anger within him. Normal males are more prone to anger and less able to control it.

This explains the rise of the Manosphere movement and the increase in violent crime from the average male. Black pill is a sector of the Manosphere where involuntary celibates promote suicide or mass killings as result of their lack of value on the planet and inaccessibility to women. The lack of the basic needs of male being met increases anger.

Patriarchy has created a society where men feel entitled to women because the laws created stripped women of their rights for a long time and forced them to depend on males. Historically, fathers owned the daughters and practically sold them to males. Modern males have grown accustomed this free access and ability to choose and select women; a privilege they were not biologically capable of possessing.

Now, the artificial society upheld by laws and law enforcement is being eroded, the male is becoming increasingly angry.

This is occurring because the male heavily depended on these laws to uphold his delusions of being the superior sex. As the superior sex, he is entitled to higher wages, sex, women, freedom and praise. This is how patriarchy conditioned the male for centuries. When reality clashes with a firmly held false belief, a psychological effect known as cognitive dissonance is produced. This effect produces a negative discordant feeling inside of the body and this feeling induces anger. Since 55% of the global population has firmly held beliefs of male god philosophies, male superiority and female inferiority, the reality of women excelling in many male dominated arenas induce anger in many males.

Inducing anger in males and driving up their testosterone is dangerous for society and world. This is how boxers are trained.

The reality is males are designed to earn everything they get in life. By giving males everything, it has effectively altered their psychology and induced a widespread of personality disorders among them.

The build up testosterone and the lack of expulsion through primitive means has aided in the the NPD trait increase among normal males.

Based on the science, males are predisposed to NPD and it only takes positive reinforcement of the characteristics to send them into full blown NPD status.

Machiavellian

Last but not least is the Machiavellian. This personality type was named after Niccolo Machiavelli, an Italian politician, who specialized in the art of being cunning, deceptive and conniving for the obtainment of money, power and status.

The male's primary nature is sex and power. Money and status are only power symbols that were artificially created by Patriarchal philosophies. This personality type is driven by the degree and intensity of the lower nature of male.

Machiavellians do not necessarily need to be the center of attention. They play the background and will play the long waiting game to get what they want from a person.

Machiavellians are much more slick and subtle than narcissists. They are the snakes of the Dark Triad. Machiavellians are obsessed with being in leadership positions because they get the access to the power that comes with the position. They will hoard and hide valuable information from others to advance themselves. They scheme without regard of what effect it will have on others. Luring and seducing a potential victim into bad behaviors or relationships is common behavioral pattern.

The Machiavellian will be your Pimps, Scammers,Politicians and Business Men. They are overly interested in Money, power and status and they will play covert positions.

If you really focus on this chapter and line up the personality traits with the intentions of each type of male, you will see that you can not escape this game of life that has been created. Males are not going to change because this is in their nature and as long as we are still operating in an unnatural matrix of societies, there will always be disorder.

Women have the power to change this reality if only they would wake up, see and accept the truth.

CHAPTER 44

NEEDS CHANGE, YOU'RE GONE

"When a man's needs change, his woman changes."
—*Princella Clark*—

To summarize this up, males are seeking to get their needs met at your expense. The only reason they are with you is because you fulfill a need. They are incapable of love therefore they can't love you. However, they do need to give you the illusion of "love" so you will willingly give yourself up. Farrakhan preached this to his congregation. "When you fall in love with a man, it makes you willing to give yourself up. Im not talking about your body. I'm talking about giving up your mind, your own aspirations, your own desires for your future. When you fall in love with a man you give your life to accept his life." In other words, destroy yourself, take on male beliefs and purposes and ensure his survival. Forget your own survival.

Here is the link for you to verify this yourself. At the 9:24 mark he speaks. https://www.youtube.com/watch?v=phi9QWhYbRw

Men deal with women based on what they need you for. Here is another link for you to verify this. Begin at the 3:50 mark to 4:04 https://www.youtube.com/watch?v=5w2Hfidm6FA&t=372s

All men have the same base needs. However, the priority changes and the rank in importance changes. No one need is better than another need. It's a need and someone has to fulfill it. When their needs change, the woman they are with changes. If you are fulfilling multiple needs, a male will not want to lose that because those needs are secured. However, he will need to "cheat" in order to get other needs met. You can not be everything he needs and you shouldn't try to be. This is what drains your life force energy. This is what ages you and stresses you out. You are here to be much more than a slave to his needs.

It does not make you any better than another woman because he wants to drain you more than he gives the impression of draining another woman. It is not that he doesn't want to drain the other woman at the same capacity. It's that she either 1. does not have the particular resource that he wants to drain. 2. She does have it but he is manipulating you into competition to get benefits from both women. 3. If she does have it, she is smart enough not to give him access to it. That, in and of itself, triggers his desire to conquer her, thus keeping him chasing. He does this while you're home slaving and making his return comfortable so he can chase again tomorrow. Seeking male validation is a low state for women.

Women hoarding resources and not giving back to the ecosystem, community, and environment is male behavior. Women have been under the brainwashing of patriarchal philosophies and environments so long that they have truly forgotten how to be women. If you are going to use the few males who have money, don't hoard the resources for yourself. Give back to the planet. Give back to society and improve life on earth for all. If he won't do it and you won't do it, who's going to do it? The ruling class who is already destroying the planet? I think not. They are destroying the planet as a viable habitat for all life. They only create the illusion they are doing "good." Please know what you give you will get back 10 fold. There's no scarcity. There's abundance when women rule.

Find Love within yourself. Stop seeking outside of yourself for something men are not capable of giving you. Become this love and save your, your daughter's lives and the planet. This is bigger than dating, this is a rise planetary consciousness and human evolution.

Love,

Princella The Queen Maker

Made in the USA
Middletown, DE
23 June 2023